Expanded Ministry to Adults:
Program Guidelines

by
Dorsey Brause

Robert A. Crandall, Ph.D., Executive Director
Dorsey Brause, Ph.D., Managing Editor
Catherine Stonehouse, Ph.D., Consulting Editor

Light and Life Press
Winona Lake, Indiana 46590

ISBN 0-89367-030-8

Printed in the United States of America by
Light and Life Press, Winona Lake, Indiana 46590

Contents

Introduction

Expanded Ministry to Adults: Program Guidelines begins with an explanation of foundational beliefs and assumptions. This gives the reader perspective. It provides direction and purpose for an expanded ministry to adults. Program objectives and activities need to be consistent with this foundation of ministry. They must contribute to the suggested mission statement, "to aid adults in the continuing process of becoming."

Expanded Ministry to Adults: Program Guidelines ends by dealing with leadership development. The conscientious leader of adults must seek ways to expand his efforts. Persons capable of leadership need to be recruited, motivated, trained, and kept. The last chapter tells how to do this.

Between the beginning and the end is included an organized "smorgasbord" of topics. These include theory; the why, and practice; the what and the how. Both are needed to assure that moments of truth occur — occasions when relevant activities for adults are implemented. This section includes explanations of many specific programs and activities.

This book is designed to be a usable resource. It is broad in scope. A wide range of programs, possible in both the small church and the large church, is included. Study of this book will help local church leaders plan and implement their expanded ministry to adults — programs beyond Sunday school and beyond the services administered by the pastor.

As you read this book "think adults," "think change," and "think gospel." Best wishes as you prepare to create and implement activities which creatively confront adults with the life-changing and life-renewing gospel.

Dorsey Brause
Author

The Foundation of Ministry

Can You
1. recite the mission statement for adult ministries?
2. name the four functions of Scripture as specified in II Timothy 3:16?
3. indicate the relationship of the local church director of adult ministries to church auxiliaries?
After studying chapter 1 you can.

An athlete may be successful without the fundamentals, but only for a short time. The farmer who plants corn must first prepare a solid seedbed. A pianist who shows great freedom and creativity of expression has mastered the fundamentals. Every soldier must first go through basic training. The Ph.D. candidate must possess a great fund of previous knowledge. Slight errors in the foundation of a building are not really apparent until the higher floors are reached. The foundational learnings a child has missed may go undetected until high school. Failure to follow some foundations of child rearing may not be apparent until later years. In all of these instances foundations may not be readily observable, but they are important, even critical.

An expanded ministry to adults must be built on a prayerfully considered foundation. Goals, programs, and activities are then identified which will be consistent with this foundation.

The building blocks are critical for this foundation of expanded ministry to adults. Such a ministry includes programs for adults beyond Sunday school and beyond the services administered by the pastor. This ministry, plus adult Sunday school classes, is the responsibility of local church directors of adult ministries. Consequently, this book is addressed to them. Others interested in leading adult programs in the church will find this book helpful. Following are these building blocks:

A Dynamic View of Adulthood

Becoming an adult is not, at age twenty-one, emerging fully grown and fully developed — like a butterfly. That is the child's view — the old view. One of the significant discoveries of this generation is that we can continue to grow and develop throughout our entire lives. In each of us there is a hidden potential, even a hidden splendor, that continues to unfold as we are nurtured and nourished through the adult years. Adults should be growing spiritually. They should be competing with their *own* past records. In specific, measurable areas of spiritual development, are they ahead compared to six months ago? a year ago? Success in the Christian life is measured by what we *are,* compared to what we *could* be!

Adults have different concerns and interests at different ages and in different circumstances. Adults are continually emerging. Adults can experience expanding physical, intellectual, spiritual, and aesthetic dimensions throughout life. Adulthood should be viewed as many different ages, each with unique concerns, interests, and attitudes. Adulthood is not stagnant. It is an expanding, enhancing, and challenging process to pursue. But, it is an individual process. However, no adult need ever be "over the hill." More appropriately one is "getting out of the woods" and viewing reality with ever-increasing clarity. Remember Browning's words, It is "the last of life, for which the first was made." Remember too, the ripe fruit is the best fruit.

The Great Adventure

An effective expanded ministry to adults should assist each person in the great adventure which is a life with Christ. An adventure may be defined as a journey of unexpected turns and events. II Corinthians 3:18 (RSV) indicates, "And we all, with unveiled face, beholding the glory of the Lord, are being changed into his likeness from one degree of glory to another; for this comes from the Lord who is the Spirit." With full access to God (unveiled face) we are being changed into the likeness of Christ. The mission statement for ministry to adults can well be "to aid adults in the continuing process of becoming."

Adults need to see God's purposes and learn how to cooperate with Him in achieving them. Included in this are His purposes for each person's life. The questions: What can God teach me in this situation? and How can I cooperate with God? are keys to effective adult living. But in this process the major purpose must be kept in mind, that is, to be "changed into his likeness." This surely includes reproducing the character of Christ in our lives and maturing as Christians. What attitude, character trait, or lesson can I learn or develop through this frustration, success, opportunity, or irritation? What can I do? How shall I perceive this life situation to cooperate with God in His making of me what He wants to make? Clearly "we are his workmanship" (Ephesians 2:10). Notice the verb "are" is continuous and ongoing. Thus our mission, "to aid adults in the continuing process of becoming." Every activity, program, and project should contribute to this mission.

Adults without Christ are hurting, because only in Christ can one put his life together. We mature in Christ only as we adopt His purposes and live as His man or woman in the situation life has dealt us under His direction. Our ministry needs to aid adults in this process, in living their "great adventure." With an unconditional commitment adults can enjoy life with God. They can be triumphant overcomers.

Needs- and Life-Centered

Any program for adults must be based on needs. Careful planning must go into any methods used to identify needs.

Christianity is practical. It always sees truth as related to life. Christianity has to do with situations "where the rubber hits the road," where the real issues of life are lived, experienced, fought, and wept over.

Adults need and want immediate application of information. They want to know: How is this relevant to my life right now; and, What has this to do with me in my situation?

The mark of the Christian is a unified life. God is God during the week as well as on Sunday. He is God in the marketplace. "He is there, and He's not silent." He's involved in the warp and woof of life. He is there where the real issues and concerns of living are experienced. For the Christian, the secular and sacred become one. Spiritual implications are seen in everything. All of life's happenings and events can be used to make us into what God would have us be. We thank God for what we are, and we also thank God for what we are becoming.

Truth

All truth anywhere of any kind is God's truth. God is the God of truth (Psalm 31:5). His Son is the Lord of truth (John 14:6). God's Spirit is the Spirit of truth (John 14:16, 17). An effective ministry to adults must have an unshakable commitment to the truth.

On occasion I've indicated to humanistic colleagues with whom I worked in the past that I'm simply a fellow traveler with them in a common human predicament. Every man's task is to find out as much as possible about the journey. His task and mine is to find the truth. Then I explain that truth is found in the biblical interpretation of the origin, purpose, meaning, and destiny of man. Truth is not a matter of opinion; it is a matter of fact. The rational man cannot be angry or argue with truth. Since God is truth, He is thus believable.

At every level, secular media and secular education influence us with the "beneath the surface" teaching that there is no God. We expect these systems to deal with the real issues and concerns of life. Since they do not include

God, many assume that either He does not exist or that He does not matter. This condition in society also tends to develop a divided life. On the one hand is Sunday, church, and spiritual matters. On the other hand is the rest of the week, earning a living, and getting on with life. Very frequently these two never meet. But the mark of the Christian is a unified life.

The Bible

II Timothy 3:16 says: "All scripture is given by inspiration of God, and is profitable for [1] doctrine, for [2] reproof, for [3] correction, and for [4] instruction in righteousness" (KJV). Doctrine contains the basic fixed principles of life which apply to everyone. These principles provide the rules for us to get along with ourselves, to get along with others, and to rightly relate to God. These doctrines (or principles) apply to us whether we believe in them or not. They apply to everyone. They are nonchanging. They are part of reality just as is the law of gravity.

Scriptures profitable for reproof are those portions which show how relationships are adversely affected when God's principles are violated. One readily thinks of David — his violation of God's principles; and the effect on his personal life, his family life, and his future career. Solomon is another person who in the latter years of his life violated God's principles. Many other illustrations are found in Scripture that relate to the adverse effect on the nation of Israel as the Israelites violated God's principles.

The third function of Scripture is for correction. This suggests the steps that can be taken to get back into right relationship with self, others, and God. This is shown in the Scriptures through the repeated cycles of God's people following God, then turning from God, then coming back to Him again through the ministry of the prophets and priests. The New Testament deals with this matter of correction as well. Certainly the point concerning a penitent and contrite heart, as being the sacrifice acceptable to God, illustrates this point.

Finally, the fourth function of Scripture is instruction in righteousness. This means that the Scriptures are useful for showing how doctrines, reproofs, and corrections are reinforced, reaffirmed, and strengthened. The doctrine, reproof, and correction themes are repeated throughout Scripture. As these themes are studied in their various settings and circumstances, quite naturally reinforcement of learning occurs. An instructor puts knowledge into new forms and settings. Scripture does likewise.

"Follow the manufacturer's directions" is good advice in caring for household appliances. It is also good advice for living a life. The Bible, as the Book of Life, contains the Manufacturer's directions.

The Priesthood of the Believer

This means direct access to God. It also means the right and privilege to offer spiritual sacrifices. It further means the responsibility to witness in the world. Every adult is to be a priest to others. He should assume responsibility to assist every person he contacts to realize his potential in Christ. It is God who creates this priesthood. As a priest the adult must be taught and motivated to seek God through the many means at his disposal. Among these are prayer, study of and meditation on God's Word, fellowship with other Christians, corporate worship, being under the authority of the Spirit, assuming responsibility in the body of Christ, and using for ministry whatever gift God has given.

The Teachable Moment

Those working with adults need to be aware of the teachable moment, when the learner is actively in search of an idea, a concept, or an experience to provide a new slant, a new skill, or a new focus for life. It might be called that brief instant in which the heart and mind of a person are open to the learning of a truth as a result of circumstances and experiences. Teachable moments exist in time of conflict or crisis when there is a feeling of inadequacy, when a need or a problem is recognized, when a goal is set, or when a person is searching for meaning in life. During a recent time of extended and unexpected hospitalization I experienced a personal crisis when I was particularly teachable. As leaders of adults, we must look for teachable moments, those times when persons say, "I need help" and thus are ready to learn.

Frequently, teachable moments occur during milestones or discriminating events in the adult life cycle. Following are some specific milestones around which teachable moments may occur: marriage, the birth of the first child, a new position or job, children flying the nest, an extended illness, reaching retirement, death of a spouse, vocational changes or relocations, marriage of children, becoming a grandparent, death of a parent, permanent disability, failure in the job, an advancement in position, or buying a new home.

Enthusiasm

Get excited yourself. If you're not stimulated by the Word, by God, by Jesus Christ, by the program that you're working with in ministering to adults, others will not be. Enthusiasm is a normal result of being possessed by God. It is contagious just like the measles. Don't bore adults when teaching God's Living Word. Don't bore adults with haphazard programs.

Involvement

The more participants are personally involved, the greater their ownership and interest in adult ministries programs. Expect persons to actively get involved. Get excited over what they do in fulfilling assignments. Get other people to promote the program rather than only the official leader. Give recognition, encouragement, and approval to those assisting you. Dale Carnegie says, "Be hearty in your praise and lavish in your approbation." Every adult likes to be noticed, made to feel that he's important and has something to contribute.

Relationship with Church Auxiliaries

In the typical church there exists a special men's group and a women's group which may be connected with the missions movement. These may be outside the direct responsibility of the director of adult ministries. The women's auxiliary may concentrate on studying its denominational missions effort and the needs of missionaries. Frequently prayer circles or couples' circles are formed. A reading program and conventions may also be a part of the women's auxiliary program. Monthly meetings, mission projects, and study emphases are further activities.

The special men's group may have prayer breakfasts in which fellowship, information, and inspiration are involved. Some men's groups emphasize personal evangelism and personal discipleship programs. District, conference, and even denominational men's group meetings may be held.

It is important to coordinate activities between adult ministries and these auxiliary organizations. Frequently, the auxiliary organizations and the adult ministries director attempt to meet the needs of the same persons. Periodic planning sessions should occur with the head of the women's and men's organizations. Informal contacts should be made between meeting times to assure effective working relationships and adequate communication.

All aspects of programs and activities to meet the needs of adults need to be integrated and coordinated. This integration and coordination is a responsibility of the local church director of adult ministries. Failure to perform this role diminishes a major advantage of the age-level approach to Christian education — to assure that there is not a duplication of effort and activities in meeting the needs of adults. Programs should not compete. They should build on each other.

Relationship with Sunday School

Sunday school contains the basic teaching program for adults. It has the elements of regular meeting times and an established format. Frequently, the grouping of adults for other activities follows that established by the Sunday school. An expanded ministry to adults must be coordinated with Sunday school programs and activities.

A Total Spectrum Curriculum

Within the church there should be a "total spectrum" adult curriculum or program. This is one that meets the needs of adults at various levels or steps of their spiritual lives. It may be implemented during Sunday school and at other times. It must motivate adults to continue their spiritual growth. My observation is that if one is not growing spiritually, such a person is regressing or losing spiritual ground. Additionally, this curriculum must equip adults for greater and greater service for Christ and the church.

Adults grow through many experiences. Spiritual and intellectual growth are continuous processes. These facts are critical to an understanding of an effective ministry to adults. Most of these growth experiences occur outside the church, but many result from church programs and activities. The church's role is to assist in integrating these, whether from within or without the church, into a personal Christian life-view.

Central to achieving that task are the adult leader's continuing personal questions. What has this curriculum content to do with my adults now in their individual life situations *and* how is it relevant? With that in mind, leadership will tend to be practical and down to earth.

First the adult needs a clear explanation of his condition outside Christ and the remedy for that. A biblically based plan of salvation should be identified and used. Additionally, you may find your denomination's salvation booklets helpful.

After an adult accepts Christ, he is ready for the discipleship role. *Born Again, Now What?* the name for a popular adult Sunday school curriculum piece, expresses the starting point for discipleship/nuturing. How to be Christian in a non-Christian world needs to be mastered by the new Christian. Topics such as the following may well be part of this nuturing/discipleship curriculum:

Basic Christian Beliefs
The Christian Life-style
Wholesome Interpersonal
   Relationships
Strategies for Vital
   Christian Living
The Christian Family

The Christian and Social
   Problems
Bible Study — John
The Complete Christian
One-on-One Relationships:
   a Sure Way to Grow
Marriage Encounter
Christian Parenting

The adult who knows who and what he is as a Christian now needs training in witnessing to others and winning them to Christ. Topics in this curriculum may well include:

The Steps to Becoming
   a Christian
Witnessing at Work
Bible Study — Acts
Christian Growth Groups
   (Small Bible Study)

Friendship/Common
   Interest Evangelism
Neighborhood Evangelism
The Marks of Cults
Living/Witnessing in
   the Home

Next, an emphasis should be made on the discovery of spiritual gifts. In the very definition of gifts, their use in the local church is implied. Consequently, identifying specific channels for such use is essential. Topics relating to the portion on gifts may include:

The Nature of the Body
   of Christ
How to Discover One's Gift(s)
The Gifts of the Spirit:
   a Biblical Perspective
Analyzing Church Tasks and
   Offices
Bible Study — I Corinthians
   12; Romans 12; I Peter 4;
   Ephesians 4 (Gifts)

Qualifications for the
   Various Church Worker/
   Leader/Officer Positions
Becoming and Growing
   Through Responsible
   Leadership in the Body
The Human Instrument
   God Uses

This "total spectrum" adult curriculum is necessary since the active church continually has persons at differing levels of personal spiritual growth. Assistance is available from your church's denominational headquarters in identifying the specific resources applicable for such a ministry to adults. Each of the various components in the cycle of new birth in Christ — nurturing/discipling, witnessing, and the use of one's gift in the body — requires a separate emphasis. An effective ministry to adults stresses all components.

Would You
1. recite the mission statement for adult ministries?
2. name the four functions of Scripture as specified in II Timothy 3:16?
3. indicate the relationship of the local church director of adult ministries to church auxiliaries?

Your Move
1. List several reasons that most adults do not personify the dynamic view of adulthood discussed in this chapter.
2. Identify the most recent instance as a believer when you performed a priestly function.
3. Define the teachable moment. Explain the circumstances when you had such a moment recently.
4. Obtain next Sunday's lesson material for an adult Sunday school class. Discover the relevance of this curriculum content for your adults by identifying from it one or more biblical principles — rules for living or expectations of God.

chapter 2
Marriage and Family Enrichment

Can You
1. explain and compare the format of two widely publicized marriage/communication enrichment programs?
2. suggest several ways to get families started in family worship?

After studying chapter 2 you can.

The chances are that thirty-eight out of one hundred new marriages will end in divorce. This is a shocking statistic. Without doubt, marriage is in trouble. Responses to the increasing disintegration of marriage and the family have been many and varied. Organizations, government agencies, and college courses dealing in marriage and family living have all come about in recent decades. Church organizations have provided increased curriculum materials, family life seminars, retreats, and family camps. In the more recent family concern programs, recognition has been given to the fact that family durability is directly related to husband and wife communication.

One widely publicized program which stresses such communication is Marriage Encounter. It is a fully developed program with years of successful use.

Marriage Encounter

Marriage Encounter was brought from Spain to the United States in 1967. The program consists of a forty-four-hour weekend experience (Friday evening to late Sunday afternoon). It is designed to make good marriages better. It breaks down barriers and enables married couples to communicate freely with their spouses. It is a weekend in which a couple can concentrate on each other in a retreat setting where other couples are doing the same thing. Children are left at home, watches and clocks removed, and jobs forgotten so that husbands and wives may concentrate on each other. Communication with persons other than one's spouse is limited to meals and small talk at general sessions.

The emphasis of the Marriage Encounter is for husband and wife to concentrate on talking deeply with each other. They build a relationship under God. The term "Encounter" in this sense means to discover, to meet again. There is no age limit. It is for all marriages.

The weekend is presented by a team of five to eight persons ("lay couples" and clergy) to a group of eight to twenty married couples. There are four phases to the program — self; we; we and God; we, God, and the world. The method of the Marriage Encounter uses the following pattern:

First, . . . a *presentation* or sharing by the team. There are twelve different talks related to the various aspects of marriage. Biblical principles related to marriage are emphasized. Each talk is followed by questions pertaining to the presentation.

Second, . . . *personal reflection:* Each person reflects on the questions and is given time to write down his personal feelings related to them.

Third, . . . *conjugal dialogue:* The couples are given time to exchange notebooks with each other. After reading what the other has written, they are to dialogue in an effort to better understand each other.

Through this, a method of communication is learned which is used after the encounter weekend is over. Consequently, couples experience the joy of seeing the great potential in their own marriage. The new commitment to God and to outreach resulting from the encounter experience aids church growth. Notice what participating couples have said about this program.

COUPLE NUMBER 1

"Our Marriage Encounter experience literally changed our lives — from the inside out. We discovered new depths of love, new and complete trust, and a wonderful new joy. But the greatest part of the weekend was the infilling of God's Spirit. We had never known it was possible to experience such overwhelming love for God and for each other."

COUPLE NUMBER 2

"Marriage Encounter was tremendous, and we shall never forget that weekend, as it was beautiful and very special. It brought a new dimension to our love for each other, for others, and, naturally, for God. It's what we have needed for years in our churches. It makes a strong bond of love and joy that can be felt. We shall never be the same.

COUPLE NUMBER 3

"A Marriage Encounter weekend is a wonderful experience. It helped us as a couple to better understand each other. Marriage Encounter *does* make a good marriage even better. We highly recommend a Marriage Encounter weekend for everyone."

Marriage Encounter is not a sensitivity group. There is no group dialogue or group dynamics; there is no manipulation by leaders. It is not a time to go over mistakes of the past. Things discussed are those that are important to the moment. What is learned is applicable to everyday life.

Marriage Encounter has been called the fastest growing religious movement in the United States and Canada today. It seems to be touching a primary hurt in most marriages. Ann Landers has stated that if she were to pick out the most important ingredient necessary for a happy marriage it would be the ability to effectively communicate. This is exactly what Marriage Encounter endeavors to accomplish in the most direct way possible. But it provides an extra. It helps to develop a relationship under God.

Contact your denominational director of adult ministries for information concerning current schedules of Marriage Encounter weekends.

Another widely publicized program which also stresses communication is the Interpersonal Communication Program (formerly called the Minnesota Couples Communication Program). This is for persons who are married or who relate through work or other relationships. The program meets weekly for four three-hour sessions. The focus is on skills or process. The couple is thought of as a system in which two people share a set of expectations of how to behave toward each other and how to maintain or modify their relationship. The goal is to help the couple increase the effectiveness of their communication by specific means. First, the couple is introduced to ways in which they can better understand their communication. Second, each couple is assisted to increase specific communication skills. The Interpersonal Communication Program is unique in that an attempt is made to help both members of a couple increase understanding and skills together.

Training is given regarding the achievement of shared meaning, that is, the speaker receives confirmation on having been understood (or misunderstood) by "feedback" from the second member of the system.

Participants concentrate on communication styles of which there are four:

Style one — Friendly, sociable, conventional, everyday, relaxed, tension free, or playful.

Style two — Directive, persuasive, demanding, evaluative, blaming, or praising.

Style three — Speculative, tentative, searching, reflecting, exploring, or intellectual.

Style four — Disclosing, explicit, responsive, accepting, and aware.

Your denomination's director of adult ministries can provide source information indicating where training programs are held. This person can also supply information concerning programs to train Interpersonal Communication Program instructors.

Some excellent pastoral teams, couples, and marriage specialists, including physicians, are available on a limited basis for retreats and conferences dealing with marriage enrichment. The format of those programs varies. Leaders typically select insights and principles from a variety of sources which they put together to form their own custom-made program. Your denominational director of adult ministries can provide the names and addresses of such leaders.

Family Life Education

Family Life Education is a responsibility of an expanded ministry to adults. The person responsible for adult ministries needs to organize, encourage, and promote a Family Life Education program in his church. The following are some ideas that can be used:
Use the Family Life Rating Scale on page 21.

This will create awareness of effective family practices and may promote their use. Use it as a bulletin insert at an appropriate time such as a Family Week emphasis.

Institute "Family Night at Home"

This is one night a week in which family members stay home together. Make this a church practice which is given extensive support. A variety of family activities can be suggested such as an overnight camp-out trip, beginning a family project, taking up a family hobby, singing together, playing a table game together. Specific activities, games, projects, or other experiences can be suggested from time to time in the church bulletin or by other means.

Family Life Rating Scale

Notice these positive Christian family practices. Rate your family by marking each item appropriately:
4 — Always; 3 — Usually; 1 — Sometimes; 0 — Never

____ Does our family have grace before each meal?

____ Are discussions about religion and the church a normal part of our conversation?

____ Do all family members express and receive unconditional love (whether they are good, bad, nice, clean, dirty, obedient, belligerent, or helpful)?

____ Do parents apologize to children when parents have acted unfairly, lost their tempers, or otherwise discredited themselves?

____ Does our family worship together each day, that is, read the Bible or material commenting on the Bible and pray?

____ Is our family budget designed to include at least the tithe, one-tenth of the income set aside for the Lord's work?

____ Do parents examine themselves to correct faults which may be a hindrance between them and their children?

____ Do our family members do things together each week, for example, participate in games, picnics, hobbies, trips, vacations, singspirations, group viewing of TV, shopping, sight-seeing, sports, bike riding?

____ Aside from times of illness, does our family attend church together at least once a week?

____ Is God involved naturally and normally at times of blessing as well as times of hardship?

____ Are the resources of God called upon to resolve the ongoing concerns of each family member (from school issues to problems at work or the office)?

____ Do all family members unite in prayer for major personal or family concerns?

____ Do family members give recognition to each other's achievements?

____ Do family members encourage each other?

____ Do family members try to communicate with and understand each other?

____ Are family members involved in spiritual outreach through witnessing, evangelizing, discipling, or counseling?

____ Is our family building a "museum of memories," that is, a series of positive experiences which will stand the test of time as being high points of togetherness?

____ Are parents united in establishing and enforcing family standards for children?

____ Do children perceive the father as the spiritual and disciplinary leader in the home?

Add the scores assigned and take heed of your rating:

76 — You're kidding, get serious
57-75 — Excellent
37-56 — Good
22-36 — Needs improvement
1-21 — Poor
0 — Impossible, no family is that bad

Emphasize Family Devotions

The family is the church in miniature. The human personality is exposed in the home as nowhere else. We are psychologically unclothed in our family relationships. The family can be called the basic unit of Christian education. For that reason, a major portion of this chapter is directed toward the spiritual development of the family.

If a family truly lives by the first commandment, "Thou shalt have no other gods before me," then all of family life will be family devotions. However, there still needs to be a time when all family members gather together to think about spiritual matters, to praise God together, and to fellowship or celebrate spiritual things. God admonished His people, the Hebrews, in forthright terms to have a three-pronged emphasis upon His word. Deuteronomy 6:6-7 provides the basis for this, "And these words, which I command thee this day, shall be in thine *heart:* and thou shalt *teach them diligently* unto thy children, and shalt *talk* of them when thou sittest in thine house, and when thou walkest by the way, and when thou liest down, and when thou risest up [italics mine]." Parents need to teach by example, through modeling, which comes out of the heart. They need to teach informally through talking. And then they need to teach diligently or to engage in formal teaching. The formal teaching, or family worship, needs to be accompanied by the other two, the talking and the modeling.

Children tend to see God or to think of God as they see and think of their father. Some children want to have little to do with God if He is like their father. They see Him as lacking love, compassion, empathy, understanding, caring, and consideration.

Children need to see that God is the most important force in the lives of the parents. They need to see that God is called upon as a resource to solve real problems: at work and in the family, problems of economics and health, problems relating to getting along with neighbors, and all other problem areas. Children need to see how God helps to overcome problems, helps to change attitudes, helps in real life situations, and provides solutions to problems.

God admonishes parents to talk to their children about His commands. This should come as family members share insights from reading the Bible or Christian literature. This informal teaching or talking can come while a parent plays ball with a child or transports a child to a school function. It can take place while parent and child are washing dishes, while working in the garden, or while at the dinner table. It may be a simple comment about the nature, characteristics, or expectations of God. It may be a casual statement related to God's standards and principles. It may be a reference to spiritual resources as a solution to a problem or concern of parent or child. It may simply be a query, What does the Bible teach about this kind of attitude?

Informal teaching also occurs when the entire family prays about a concern of a child or parent. This praying and sharing of insights might be about Daddy's boss at work. It may be about a change of vocation or job for Daddy or Mother. (All my several job changes have been a total family prayer concern and have been made only after all members have agreed.) It may be praying about Johnny's imminent visit to the dentist. It may be a family prayer focus and concern on Susie's problems with English. The focus may be Johnny's tryout or participation in Little League baseball. You see, the sharing and praying are directed toward, and come naturally out of, the family life-style. The base of that life-style is belief in God. It is obedience to the first of the Ten Commandments, "Thou shalt have no other gods before me." Thus, the family together calls upon God, looks to God, and lets God speak to them about real concerns.

The Deuteronomy passage indicates that God's words are to be taught diligently. This refers to the more formal family worship which should occur in the home. This formal worship should occur regularly, hopefully every day, and may consist of various forms. However, it should contain the elements of devotional reading, with at least some direct reference to Bible verses and prayer. Singing, memorizing, discussing, and sharing of significant events are other components. The family needs to keep in mind the reasons for effective family worship. The following can be outcomes of family worship which is pursued with intelligence and spiritual discernment:

1. It unites the family in the highest endeavor known to man, that is, worship of God.
2. It is a natural response to God for His gift of life. It is also a natural response to the first commandment.
3. It strengthens the family members in their faith. It strengthens their commitment to Jesus Christ.
4. It is a reminder that God is in first place in this family.
5. It is a time when prayer is learned.
6. It creates an atmosphere of reverence or sanctity of life.
7. It dissolves or resolves family misunderstandings. It improves family life. It resolves tensions among family members. Family members cannot pray together if they have spite or bitterness.
8. It develops a reservoir of very precious memories and shared experiences which are very important for both family and personal stability.
9. When observed, it is a witness to other persons outside the family.

Family worship should be adjusted to the age levels of children and it should be child centered. Excellent graded devotional books appropriate for children at various age levels are available from your denominational publisher.

Now how do you get families started in family worship? The following are some ways that work:

1. Emphasize the significance of grace at meals. Stress that this is really recognizing the presence of Christ in their midst. It's more than affirming good fortune in having enough to eat. Grace is a profound symbol of the family's place in the kingdom of God. It is a reminder that God has first place. Suggest that routine grace be expanded to

include a more personal recognition of God's presence. Suggest that grace might be a time of thanks or intercession for other aspects of family life rather than just the food before them.

2. Emphasize family worship during a family month or family week churchwide emphasis. Provide some guidelines for this. Among these guidelines may be verses, devotional readings, and a devotional book which is graded for different ages. The guides may include songs to sing and some of the suggestions contained in this chapter.

3. The pastor or Sunday school teacher may request that a family pray for an aspect or component of his ministry. Perhaps the request might be for prayer before the family leaves for church. This may be the beginning of family worship.

4. Perhaps giving families a devotional book may be the trigger that gets them to engage in family worship.

5. A family may engage in its first family worship in relation to a significant family event, such as a death, a wedding, a birthday, the baptism of a family member, the beginning of a school term, a family crisis, or some other major experience. Family worship may begin in regard to a special day, such as Thanksgiving or Christmas. It may be short, but it must be real.

6. Print prayer requests in church bulletins or on special attractive prayer request cards to be picked up or distributed. This may help families to begin praying together.

7. When a pastor or director of adult ministries requests to visit a family, he may suggest that he would like to draw the family together for family worship. This may be a first experience for the family from which family worship may become traditional.

8. Family worship may occur the first time when a family dedicates a Christmas bundle prepared for

foreign relief. Or it might occur when a family assumes responsibility for part of a Sunday evening service or a service at a community rest home. Those working in adult ministries can plan such events and suggest that their implementation be preceded by family worship.

9. Periodically have different families demonstrate family devotions to the local church body. This should be done with families having children of different age levels, both boys and girls. Part of a Sunday evening service could be used for this purpose.

10. Distribute suggestions for family worship that can be used over and over such as those on pages 27 and 28.

Other Ideas for Family Life Ministry:

Feature a Book of the Month

This is a book on family living that all members of the congregation are urged to buy and read. Then set aside a Sunday evening to discuss it. Have your pastor or another person make a fifteen- to twenty-minute presentation on the book. Then divide into small groups of ten to twelve persons to discuss it. Have persons with the most recent birthdays lead the groups or identify others to do so.

Establish a "Family Center" in Your Church Library

Feature books that children and parents can read together, as well as family inventories and evaluation tools. You might also have a cassette tape section dealing with family concerns.

Pair Up Church Families for Visitation

Divide your church into pairs of families based on members' compatibility of personalities and ages. Have one family visit another for an hour-and-a-half devotional and sharing time. The host family plans the evening, and the visiting family of one week will become the host of the next. Use bulletin inserts to suggest things families can do

Repeatable Family Worships

Celebration

(Scripture: Psalm 150; Philippians 4:6, 7; I Thessalonians 5:16-18)

Each family member shares the most interesting experience he has had during the past twenty-four or forty-eight hours. This may be a good thing that has happened, something that was learned, a success, an opportunity for helping or serving someone, an incident involving another person, a time of fun, a good feeling. As part of the sharing, each person explains why he categorized it as the most interesting experience.

From this positive setting, this celebration of life, the leader directs the thinking to the Author of life. Did you make yourself? Can you change much about yourself, even to adding "one cubit to your stature"? God made you as *you* — unique, different from any other — and He prescribed certain things about you. All of life is to be lived in joyous response to His gift of life.

Next, the leader directs the family in an expression of appreciation to God for these positive experiences. This might be a prayer by one family member, several, or all family members. On occasion it might be a thank-you letter to God that all family members help write or a part of which is written by each family member. At other times it may be a poem, ode, or psalm of thanks.

Spiritual Bench Marks

(Scripture: Philippians 3:1-14; II Peter 3:18; I Corinthians 10:13; Psalm 42:1)

Could it be that in totally committing our lives to Christ, we will be the losers? We answer, "No! No! No!" At least our mind answers that way because we have been taught accordingly. But our will is not always that convinced. Getting to know God better should have our best efforts. It brings more joy, delight, and contentment than does anything else. Do you pant after God as you do after other things?

Ask each family member to share a recent spiritual insight (an understanding, victory, appreciation) or problem (concern, shortcoming, sin, temptation). Make these benchmarks for the individual; that is, make them definite points of spiritual progress. Purpose to cherish and nurture each insight. For each problem, establish a goal which will solve it. As all family members are witnesses to these purposes and goals, they are to encourage each other in them during the days ahead. Thank God for them and pray that the Holy Spirit will assist.

The Relevant God

(Scripture: Psalm 121; Hebrews 13:5-8; James 1:1-16; Psalm 23)

Family members should seek God's direction in all things. God should be involved in the daily affairs of each person. This results in a diminished contrast between Sunday, church, and spiritual matters versus day-to-day living and getting along in the world. God wants to be there where "the rubber hits the road," where the real issues and concerns of living are experienced. He wants our fellowship. He wants to know us. He wants to help. We need to involve God through prayer, not just to get favors from Him but to know His mind relating to our concerns. This is the key to the dynamic Christian life; a fellowship/relationship with God.

Identify one or more real life concerns of family members. Discuss what spiritual lessons might be learned from the conditions, circumstances, or frustrations related thereto. Then discuss what might be the Christian solution to each concern. Finally, have family members pray for the resolution of each concern consistent with God's plan for the person involved.

God's Word

(Scripture: Proverbs 2:1-8; Psalm 1, 119:97; John 8:31, II Timothy 3:16)

"Follow the manufacturer's directions" is a good rule. But do you ever have trouble believing the directions that God, the manufacturer, gives for your life? God says, "Meditate on my words day and night," but we say, "Surely one chapter a day should keep me on the right track!" God says, "Love your enemies . . . pray for them," but we say, "The less I see of that person, the happier I'll be!" He says, "Pray about everything . . . ," but we say, "I've been worried about this for days." God's directions are true and available. God expects us to use His Word. Let it speak to you. Think of your problems and concerns as you meditate upon His Word. Look for healing and solutions in Scripture. Insights, understandings, and attitudes that help will come.

Find a scripture that speaks to at least one family member. Share what it means and then, as a family, memorize it together. For example, if it is Ephesians 3:16, the leader states the first word, "That," and the others repeat it. Then the leader states the first two words, "That he," and the others repeat them. Continue in this manner through the entire scripture portion, and by that time family members are well on their way to having it memorized. Now have each person print a copy of the scripture in a form which he can carry with him at all times. Ask family members, during the next twenty-four hours, to meditate upon the scripture selected, to visualize it, to personalize it, and to filter their experiences/concerns through it. Share the effects of this at the next family worship.

for devotions and sharing during these times.

Have a Family Vacation Bible School

You may want to utilize family clusters in this programming. These are groups of twelve to fifteen persons including one or more nuclear families plus senior adults and singles. Clusters worship and engage in relational activities as a group. Contact your denominational director of adult ministries for cluster family programming ideas.

Emphasize May as Family Month

Programming ideas are available from denominational headquarters.

Use Moral Issues and Sex Education Materials

Your denomination has these resources specially prepared and available for your use. Contact denominational headquarters.

Use the Teachable Moment, "Birth of the First Child"

At such times couples are responsive to the claims of Christ and His church. They want to be good parents. Classes and/or materials should be available to such couples on Christian parenting and child rearing.

Would You
1. explain and compare the format of two widely publicized marriage/communication enrichment programs?
2. suggest four ways to get families started in family worship?

Your Move
1. Complete the Family Life Rating Scale on page 21. Ask other members of your family to do likewise and compare results. (If you are a single adult ask members of a nuclear family in your church to complete the scale, compare results among them-

selves, and give their impressions of the scale's usefulness.)
2. List the three most important of the nine reasons given for effective family worship.
3. "Pair Up Church Families for Visitation" is listed on page 26 as an idea that can be used in a family life ministry. Prepare suggestions for things families can do for devotions and sharing during one such visit.

Nurture and Outreach

Can You
1. identify a nurturing strategy that can be implemented in the smallest church, assuming it has two or more adults of the same sex?
2. describe a way to encourage your adults to use their recreational interests to share Christ?
3. name several objectives of a tape ministry?
After studying chapter 3 you can.

My pastor informed me that "Layman's Sunday" was my problem. This was true, he explained, because I was president of the men's group. Traditionally, that person was in charge of the morning worship service on Layman's Sunday. I decided to involve the other men, and then contacted the first man. I explained that he had an "opportunity" — to participate with eleven other men. Each would speak for two minutes either on a significant spiritual experience he had had during the past year or on what it meant to him to be a Christian. The next person was presented with the same "opportunity" and was informed that one man had accepted. And on I went. It wasn't difficult to get twelve men to make such a presentation. I only moderated the program. It was remarkable how these men testified to their growth through this experience. Even the wives thanked me, since their husbands benefited so greatly. That day I learned of one excellent means of spiritual nurture. A simple structure for getting people to publicly share their faith can produce spiritual growth.

Nurture and outreach comprise a needed dual thrust for an effective expanded ministry to adults. Nurture refers to spiritual growth. Outreach refers to new birth in Christ. And our responsibility extends from spiritual birth to spiritual maturity. Note the following nurture and outreach strategies.

Mentor-Shepherds

The use of mentor-shepherds is a means of promoting the spiritual growth of adults. Each adult being nurtured is made the special assignment of such a person. The mentor-shepherd is:

A model of what adulthood is about, what personhood means, and what discipleship is like.

A warm, accepting, and congenial person; one who is easy to talk to; a good listener; nonjudgmental; yet one who is honest and open about personal needs, feelings, and values.

One who cares, guides, warns, protects, and reaches out to adults without imposing or nagging.

Sensitive, available and willing to spend time with adults, celebrating victories and empathizing with disappointments.

Well-grounded biblically, theologically, and psychologically; a "together person" who has explored his faith and values and therefore feels at home with himself.

What can the church do to facilitate the relationship between the new Christian and the mentor-shepherd? First of all, a mentor-shepherd is not forced upon anyone. He or she is chosen by the adult. However, it is difficult for some new Christians to know persons well enough to actually choose those who might serve well in this capacity. Thus the church needs to be about the business of developing mentor-shepherds and helping new Christians to become aware of them. The church can provide opportunities for persons in their forties and fifties and some older persons to explore the duties and ministry of being a mentor-shepherd. The church may provide opportunities for such persons to get together for study, prayer, and personal growth experiences. These persons then can begin to reach out, get acquainted, fellowship, and spend time with new Christians where the mentor-shepherd relationship might eventually develop.

Family Pairing

The pairing of fringe families with established church families is an additional way to promote nurturing. Develop a program whereby established families are given opportunity to select a fringe family for nurturing. Simply the existence of such a program may be sufficient motivation for an established family to take on such a responsibility. Exchanging home visits and engaging together in a variety of family activities are effective ways to introduce the Christian life-style to fringe families. Through these means, modeling can occur and doors can open for verbal witnessing.

One-on-One Relationships

Many Christian adults can profit from a mutual nurturing relationship with another person. A one-on-one nurturing relationship is one whereby two spiritually mature Christians of the same sex relate to each other in a meaningful fashion over an extended period of time. The relating should occur during an activity each person would be doing anyway. Thus, extra time from an already busy schedule is not required. The activity should be of such nature that uninterrupted dialogue can occur — such as exercise walks or noon luncheons.

My experience has been with noon luncheons. While a community college administrator, I ate lunch each Tuesday with the chief engineer of a local manufacturing firm. We did this for months, and we both looked forward to these meetings. Before we began, we knew we would be opening our lives to each other. We knew we would minister to each other by seeking each other's spiritual help concerning our real problems, concerns, and hurts. We expected to get involved at the center, rather than just the fringes, of each other's lives. From the beginning we knew our times together would be characterized by sharing, caring, and counseling. We expected to pray together. We expected to share scripture and encourage each other in memorization. And our sessions turned out just that way. Here's what you could do if you want to promote such interaction among the adults in your church:

1. Inform your adults about one-on-one nurturing relationships. Distribute the above two paragraphs to them or make an oral presentation at a time and place approved by your pastor.

2. Get the names, phone numbers, occupations, and places of employment of those interested.

3. Personally contact those expressing an interest and make suggestions for pairings which you believe are appropriate. Factors such as compatibility of personality, level of education, and acceptable meeting times and locations should be considered. However, benefits can accrue from mixing vocational categories and ages.

4. Follow up by checking on pairings to assure they have been meeting. Encourage those who may be slow in starting.

Common Interest Evangelism

Adults should participate in the church's regular visitation program. They should also witness to their neighbors, their "nigh-dwellers." Finally, persons at work, in the service club or social group, and those who are met in normal day-to-day pursuits should see Christ presented in an attractive manner through the adults of your church.

Do the adults use their recreational interests to introduce persons to Christ? Frequently such activities can be shared with non-Christians. Persons who share common-interest experiences develop strong relationships. This opens the door to evangelism.

Through my nearly two decades of enjoying tennis and skiing, deep relationships have developed with liberals, evangelicals, agnostics, and avowed atheists. Sometimes the terms "tennis evangelism" and "skiing evangelism" were descriptive of my major purposes since I found these to be effective means of witnessing for Christ.

I remember a frequent tennis opponent, an atheist, whose marriage was breaking up. Following a match one afternoon, he shared the deep love he had for his wife and children. He told me how he was hurting, and I told him how Jesus could meet his needs. This provided an opportunity to explain how Christ and His teachings are relevant to family concerns. We discussed the great happiness and security I had in my family, but I pointed out that without Christ, my family could well have been breaking up, too.

The Christian is not a hedonist, one who views pleasure as life's highest good and life's chief end. Rather, the Christian's response to the delightfulness and pleasures of life is one of gratitude. And this gratitude is focused on the Creator. Reference to God is logical during shared times of enjoying a recreational interest. The Christian sees God in his pleasures. And in gratitude he naturally thinks of His attributes: power, wonder, presence, beauty, praiseworthiness, awe, order, majesty, intelligence, creativity, purpose, and love.

Conversation with a non-Christian with whom you are sharing a common interest will normally reflect your current interests and concerns. How natural then to tell of the Christian book you are reading, the pastor's sermon outline, or the relevant points of your Sunday school lesson. Your comments will be accepted in the friendly conversational mill along with last night's party or sports event. However, be certain during these times to lovingly listen to your non-Christian partner's concerns.

Jesus used figures of penetration to describe the role of the Christian in the world. He said that we are to be as light, leaven, water, and salt. To carry out His teachings, we should permeate society, including recreational pursuits. Our lives are to speak normally and naturally of Him. We communicate who He is, the extent of His involvement in our lives, and the love, joy, peace, abundance, and power He brings.

To make common interest evangelism an outreach force in your church, you will want to:

1. Identify the persons you want to motivate to work at this activity. They may be your entire adult membership, a Sunday school class, or another group representing only part of the adult membership. Remember that often all that is needed is for persons to see the possibilities in an activity. You are to provide the vision and suggest that members engage in common interest evangelism.

2. List the recreational interests of those in the group. These may be hobbies, athletics, or even coffee klatches. Any activity is appropriate that can be done by more than one person — from macrame to bird-watching, from bowling to quilting — as long as it provides the opportunity to share.

3. Meet with the group. This may be as the feature or program for a regular meeting of the group. During this time:

   a. Present the rationale (create the vision) for common interest evangelism. Convey the above insights. Stress that *any* recreational interest which has the potential for involving non-Christians can be used.

   b. Discuss the specific possibilities for common interest evangelism for the persons present. Let individuals make suggestions.

   c. Provide information on how to witness more effectively. Be prepared to instruct the group on this topic including the steps in leading a person to Christ. Use *The Four Spiritual Laws* or the salvation booklets recommended by your denomination.

   d. Distribute copies of the list of personal characteristics on page 37 and discuss each.

4. Follow up with your group. Periodically remind members to think "tennis evangelism," "fishing evangelism," or "shopping evangelism."

5. Share results in three months or so. Provide

opportunity at a meeting of the group for members to:

a. Describe occasions for witnessing.

b. Describe methods used in witnessing.

c. Describe results or responses to witnessing. How many persons were nurtured? How many accepted the Lord?

d. Share how they have grown spiritually through common interest evangelism.

6. Periodically and discreetly recognize those who are effectively engaging in common interest evangelism. This will encourage them and motivate others.

As one normally and naturally shares Christ out of his life experiences, he should practice the following personal characteristics:

An open personality
You listen, weigh the evidence, and consider alternate views.

A nonshockable attitude
Regardless of what's said or done, God knows all about it.

Graciousness
God chose to give man the choice to accept or reject Him. Therefore, you can't force Jesus on anyone. Don't try.

Love
This is without condition. Jesus loved and died for even the most despicable person.

Tolerance
Don't force on others your own particular way to Christ.

Boldness
Don't be apologetic. If you have Jesus you're a winner, an overcomer. "By him all things consist" (Colossians 1:17). Jesus had a strong comment about those ashamed of Him. See Mark 8:38.

Positiveness
You know how things will turn out. Jesus will triumph. Sooner or later, every knee will bow to Him.

Humility
You're a "beggar showing another beggar where to find bread." Dwight L. Moody remarked as he observed a drunk in a Chicago gutter, "But for the grace of God, there be I."

A serving spirit
Jesus indicated that the criterion for greatness is servanthood.

A caring person
Watch for the point of need. Your non-Christian friend will more readily respond when he's hurting.

A Tape Ministry

Cassette tapes can be used in several ways to minister. Tape recordings can be made of church sermons. These can be taken to shut-ins, to those who are in the hospital, and to senior adults unable to get to church. In this way, these persons can experience being part of the ongoing church family.

Another way to use tapes is to create a listening tape ministry. Tapes of well-known Bible expositors can form the basis of a church group's ongoing program of spiritual nurture. With the widespread availability of cassette players, Christian publishers have produced listening tapes on a wide variety of subjects. People have been won to Christ and have achieved spiritual milestones through the inspiration, motivation, and teaching received in a listening tape ministry.

What are the objectives of such a ministry?

1. To expose hearers to well-known successful communicators of the gospel, to win people to Christ, to nurture those in the kingdom toward "a greater degree of likeness" to Christ.
2. To provide a relaxed, open, and comfortable setting, different from that possible during formal church services, for consideration of the gospel message.
3. To provide opportunity for discussion and personal application of biblical principles and insights.
4. To provide a Christian base for socializing, engaging in fellowship, enjoying refreshments, and participating in recreation.

Follow these guidelines as you plan and implement a listening tape ministry:

- Involve participants in selecting the tapes for listening.
- Provide opportunity to take notes.
- Do not hesitate to stop and discuss sections as the tape progresses. Replay significant portions.
- The atmosphere and activities should be non-

threatening to participants; that is, initially they should not have required responsibilities.

- Opportunities should be provided for participants to share the effects of applying biblical truths in their lives.
- Although rigid structure is to be avoided, a leader should be identified for each session to assure that it progresses and that discussion occurs.
- Participants should be encouraged to invite outsiders, thus providing an outreach dimension.
- Socializing, fellowship, refreshments, and recreation should be in keeping with the time allowed and the interests of the participants.

Alternating weekly sessions between the homes of two couples is one format that works effectively. Conversations well into the early morning hours may sometimes follow these listening sessions. They provide an excellent springboard for the application of biblical principles to personal concerns. Sessions will usually provide an atmosphere conducive to personal counseling.

Warning should be given that, at first, some persons may not be interested in listening, even to highly successful gospel communicators. Including the components of fellowship, recreation, refreshments, and socializing will help to overcome such reluctance. These components need not be highly organized. They should reflect the interest of the group.

Tapes which are purchased may be put into a collection or tape library for others to use. Some may want tapes for individual use. These may include shut-ins, sick persons, or the elderly. Persons who travel extensively by car will find listening to Christian tapes an uplifting experience. If the cost of tapes to one person should prove to be excessive, participants may share through small donations.

Ask God to give you discernment concerning the needs of persons you want to serve, and appropriate ways to meet those needs. Seek His help in promoting and making invitations for the first session. Pray for each session and pray before listening to each tape.

Several free loan libraries of cassette tapes containing Bible messages are in existence. Contact your denominational director of adult ministries for recommendations.

Drama

Drama is an excellent vehicle for spiritual growth. We are all familiar with the use of drama in celebrating the Christian festivals of Easter and Christmas. Drama can also be used to study the motivations and actions of biblical personalities and religious leaders. It can be a means to communicate biblical truths to others. Those participating in drama gain new insights and appreciation of historical and spiritual roots. Observing a drama may be the means of conveying insights to observers that no other means can achieve.

Great advances have been made in improving interpersonal skills through the use of drama. Fellowship has been greatly enhanced among the actors. I've seen persons literally change from introversion to extroversion during the several weeks involved in preparing and presenting a dramatic production. Actors must cooperate together in presenting a drama. This builds cohesiveness in the group. Participants learn to appreciate each other. They grow spiritually through this common, cooperative endeavor.

The script for dramas may be written or purchased. In either instance, when the presentation is of high quality, it should be shared with other groups. Nursing homes, other churches, and community centers are potential locations for sharing.

Music

Music as another dimension of adult ministries is a means by which man expresses his gratitude to God. Music is a joyful statement of man's attitudes. It is a means by which people express their beliefs. Much theology and doctrine is contained in the hymns of our church. The mood of a hymn may lead one either to meditation or to changed attitudes or behaviors. The singing of hymns may touch the emotions of persons. It can lead them toward dedication and a deeper commitment to the cause of Christ.

Thus, the choice of hymns for the worshipers and the choir is important. The choice of a wrong hymn may contradict the purpose of the lesson or religious experience you want your adults to have. A hymn's mood and words must be consistent with the aims and the total experience projected for the worshipers. Of course, the hymns chosen must be consistent with our faith.

Choral Speaking

Choral speaking is a pleasing alternative to one who cannot sing beautifully. Choral speaking offers a new experience in understanding and enjoyment. This is an uplifting experience to anyone who loves great literature, the sound of words, and the noble expression of fine thought. Choral speaking uses many techniques known to the singing choir. Choral speaking offers the additional freedom of not being bound by the measures of printed music. Frequently, rich hidden meanings in the words come out as first one interpretation and then another is tried.

Choral speaking can be used for a psalm or for a poem which a group has written. This action will give it deeper meaning for them. By speaking it chorally, a group effectively communicates the thoughts of the psalm or poem to others in a beautiful setting that good words deserve.

Choral speaking has the value of involving shy persons. They can participate freely without concern. Through speaking with others, they lose the fright of their own voices.

How does the adult leader who wants to use this technique begin? Start your group with a well-known selection. Adults may have as much fun as children saying, "Humpty-Dumpty sat on a wall." Listen as your adults speak this rhyme. Engage in fun and laughter as this is experienced. Nothing is as good as laughter to free and unite a group. Then you may want to try other nursery rhymes. As you progress, try marking the tempo with your hand and keeping the voices together. You may then try a selection which asks questions and provides answers. Divide the group into two parts without any attempt to locate voices. One group would ask the questions, and the other group provide the answers. Thus, you have begun. Now you may want to use choral speaking for a psalm. As this is done, notice how the words take on new meaning. Perhaps even words not discovered before are identified. Many of the psalms are meant to be used antiphonally. Remember, your purpose is to stimulate thinking as well as to speak beautifully. Let everyone have opportunity to suggest an interpretation of both the contents and the way it is to be spoken. Use the emphasis most people agree on and the interpretation which is favored, assuming, of course, doctrinal standards are upheld.

Athletics

Church athletic teams for adults can be an effective means for outreach. One pastor indicates that the use of such teams is his major means of church growth. An athletic team (softball, basketball, or volleyball) requires cooperation among participants. A sense of unity and group spirit is evident as the team competes with others. Prayer before contests can be a means of spiritual growth. During their associations together, team members can witness to each other concerning their life-styles.

Puppetry

Your adults may want to have a ministry with puppets. This can be a form of communication to reach certain individuals that may not be reached otherwise. A puppet program needs to be carefully prepared. Writing the dialogue among puppets to convey particular meanings can be a growing spiritual experience. An increased commitment to spiritual matters can result in the lives of those who conduct this ministry. One person or several may be involved in presenting the actual puppet show. Frequently, teens join adults in a puppet ministry, and both benefit.

Ministry to the Institutionalized

Adults can have an effective outreach ministry through programs conducted in jails, rest homes, and other places where persons are confined. Many churches have persons or groups who assume these responsibilities on a rotating basis. This provides more people the spiritual benefits of ministering in this fashion. It also provides a variety for those who are ministered to. Programs at these places must contain special features to meet the somewhat unusual needs of these persons. Christ needs to be presented as a practical source of hope, inspiration, and meaning. Group singing, instrumental and vocal solos, dramatic presentations, skits, choral readings, illustrated sermons, prayer, and scripture reading are means for achieving your purposes at such times.

Outreach in Educational Institutions

Some of the adults who are educators may be motivated to assume responsibility for organizing Christian groups at colleges and high schools. I have personally led such at both types of institutions. This can be done legally; but first, administrators must understand your purposes and respect your personal orientation, common sense, and cooperativeness. Bible study, prayer, outreach, discussions, and special projects, if conducted in the appropriate setting, are all legitimate activities of these organizations. The group I sponsored in a New Jersey community college organized and implemented a "Messiah Week." This was a week-long total campus emphasis. Noon activities included seminars, lectures, mini-concerts by Christian musicians, and a special debate, *"Resolved: Jesus Christ Is the World's One Messiah."* This debate generated considerable interest which was not limited to the student body. Many persons came to campus that day especially for this event.

The Home Department

The home department is one meaningful area of adult Christian education. Many churches will find individuals on their responsibility list who are not being served because of illness or some other form of disability. These persons need to be ministered to in their homes. Home department workers can promote home Bible study, distribute listening tapes and Sunday school literature by mail or personal visit, and periodically call in each home. Home department personnel may also contact shut-ins not on the church's responsibility list. These persons should be referred to the pastor.

Social Concerns

Christian social concerns are a dimension of adult ministries. For example, John Wesley, the founder of Methodism, was concerned both about the social dimensions of religion and about personal salvation. He worked with coal miners in England to better their conditions. He was much interested in people's health, and he even set up a free dispensary. Homes for widows and orphans were established. He received offerings which he distributed to the poor and to those who sought to develop small businesses of their own. He openly opposed the British slave traffic. He exhorted against drunkenness and the use of intoxicating liquors. Most churches, whether subscribing to the Wesleyan tradition or not, have given a great impetus to social concerns. Adult ministries should take the initiative in planning educational programs which come to grips with social issues. These programs should lead participants to engage in action designed to alleviate their adverse effects.

Scripture Memorization

Memorization of God's Word is a worthy dimension of adult ministries. I have personally discovered the transforming power of the Scriptures through the discipline of memorization. Adults are not excused from memorizing on the basis of their minds being less adept and elastic than they were formerly. This simply is not true. The adult can memorize. The major problem is the adult's willful lack of discipline rather than any diminishing mental ability.

The value of memorization does not come from a mechanical kind of repetition; it comes from the discipline of learning which has embedded God's truth in the mind. That truth changes attitudes, and changed attitudes in turn change conduct. We do have control over what goes into our minds and hearts. Lives have been dramatically changed through the memorization of God's Word. That is what God said would happen. If we want to think God's thoughts after Him, we need to hide God's Word in our hearts. God's Word and principles are dynamic to me. They speak to me in different conditions. They spoke to me as a child and as a young man with vastly different understanding from that I now possess. His words speak to me now. I am in my best and most rational condition when I am praying, reading the Word, or meditating upon Scripture.

Adults should select verses to memorize which personally speak to them. These verses should be personalized; that is, they should be thought of as applying specifically to the individual. They should be visualized; that is, the person should form mental images of the objects with which the verses deal. As persons meditate or think upon the verses they have memorized, they should filter their experiences, concerns, and problems through these verses. By filtering, I mean thinking of their experiences, concerns, or problems in light of these verses.

The Holy Spirit gives insights and creates attitudes, consistent with God's standards, which enable persons to cope triumphantly in the particular life situation God has permitted to come to them. Memorizing, meditating, personalizing, and visualizing meaningful scripture is an activity through which God surely blesses and causes one to grow spiritually. A program of Bible memorization, with periodic encouragement, is one that can bless your adults.

Would You
1. identify a nurturing strategy that can be implemented in the smallest church, assuming it has

two or more adults of the same sex?
2. describe a way to encourage your adults to use their recreational interests to share Christ?
3. name several objectives of a tape ministry?

Your Move
1. Identify several adults in your church who could serve as mentor-shepherds.
2. Think of several people whom you personally might win to Christ through common interest evangelism.
3. Study the Psalms and identify one which can be used antiphonally.
4. Write a scripture which you've identified as meaningful on a three-by-five-inch card. Carry it with you until it is memorized. Then twice daily for a week meditate upon it, personalize it, visualize it, and filter your experiences, concerns, and problems through it. At the end of the week, tell someone else about the blessings you've received.

Supportive Activities

Can You

1. identify the values of play in a ministry to adults?
2. describe workable devotions for a picnic using the special features of the out-of-doors?
3. name six or more kinds of retreats?
4. indicate the most relevant kind of camping for adults?

After studying chapter 4 you can.

A Christian educator recognized as a leader throughout the United States and Canada conducted a survey in which he asked adults the major reasons they go to church. He reported that their answer was: fellowship. Television supplied challenging sermons. Radio featured outstanding Bible expositors. But through those means they still failed to experience fellowship. Fellowship in a Christian context is three-sided — you, me, and the Holy Spirit. This is very special. A few years ago a friend of mine remarked about the church we both attended. He said, "Every time I go to church it's like going to a big family reunion. Everyone asks how I'm doing and how I feel; they ask about my health and how my work is coming."

What a beautiful observation. The church needs to be a place where people find and enjoy fellowship. This fellowship can develop informally even before and after worship services. Ushers and greeters can have a major influence in the level of friendliness which a church conveys. Laymen can be encouraged to be outgoing and accepting of newcomers. This contributes substantially to a "warm church," one where people experience fellowship.

Much of adult ministry deals with discipleship, nurture, evangelism, and direct spiritual growth experiences. Other legitimate ministries for adults include fellowship experiences, recreation, social functions, service, camping, and retreats. These latter may be called supportive activities. They support the more direct and obvious ministry components oriented toward the teaching/learning process. Supportive activities have a valuable role in a total ministry to adults.

Fellowship/Recreational Activities

All ages need relief from boredom, relaxation from tensions, and the self-fulfillment found in recreation. Through play, many of our most pleasant associations with other people take place. Adults should be regularly involved in recreation, fellowship activities, and social functions.

Play breaks down barriers. When persons play together they learn about each other. Hidden corners of personality are revealed. Shared laughter creates a bond between persons. We want persons in our group to grow. To do this we must know them and establish a friendly relationship with them. Play is not the only way, but it is a good way to accomplish this.

Fellowship will flourish through a wide range of activities including the following: progressive dinner, pig roast, party at a local tennis club, fellowship supper preceding church business meeting, scavenger hunt, swimming party, singspiration in a church member's home, periodic fellowship hours following morning worship, party in a home with parlor games, carol singing at the homes of shut-ins, an old-fashioned softball game, volleyball, open gym night at a local school or college, kite flying, New Year's Eve party, sweetheart banquet, stunt and skit night, Halloween costume party, all-church picnic, weiner roast, and hayride. The types of fellowship and recreational activities for adults are limited only by one's imagination and creativity.

The following are two fellowship/recreational activities which are sure winners.

"What if . . . I would . . . ?" Divide your group into two sides. Have them line up facing each other or preferably, have the two sides sit across from each other, individual by individual. On one side, each person will write and complete a question starting with "What if . . .?" On the opposite side, each person will write and complete a sentence starting with "I would. . . ." These are to be written independently and secretly. Then in turn these should be read alternately. The first person will read his question starting with "What if. . . ?" The person directly opposite will answer by reading his sentence starting with the words "I would. . . ." This continues with persons alternating sides so as to have a question followed by an answer, until each person has participated.

Pencil Charades. Divide into two groups. Take turns having one from each group communicate a song title by drawing on a sheet of paper. (No verbal communication is allowed.) The leader whispers the song title simultaneously to the two who will draw. The side which guesses the title first wins. Score is kept by counting the times each side wins. Song categories may be used such as hymns, folk songs, Westerns, old-timers, and so forth.

The All-Church Picnic

An all-church picnic can do much to develop fellowship within your church. Promote this as a major social event. Be sure everyone knows it is for them. Make your plans early enough to assure a suitable location for the picnic and lots of publicity.

In reserving a site, be sure there is an adequate location for eating and open spaces for games. Check on restroom facilities. Check on refrigeration. Select a site appropriate for the elderly. It is preferable if you can have the area to yourselves.

Plan your picnic with purposes in mind, such as (a) to develop cross-family and cross-generational fellowship and (b) to provide a spiritual experience in the out-of-doors. Assign a person to provide equipment for sports and another person to organize and implement cross-generational games.

Devotions at an all-church picnic should take advantage of the special features of the out-of-doors. They should differ from the normal Bible reading/lecture. Devotions should build group fellowship as well as provide inspiration. Here is an idea that works:

Explain the dramatic setting of Deuteronomy 27 and 28, which occurred shortly after the Israelites crossed the Jordan River. Six tribes stood on Mount Gerizim to bless the people (Deuteronomy 27:12); six stood on Mount Ebal to curse (Deuteronomy 27:13). Stress the significance of this event to the Israelites. Celebrate this great national act of commitment in the out-of-doors through an antiphonal reading.

Divide persons into east and west groups. Give each person in one group (Mount Gerizim) a copy of the eight blessings from Deuteronomy 28:3-9, 13 (KJV). Give each person in the other group (Mount Ebal) a copy of the eight curses from Deuteronomy 27:15-19 and 24-26 (KJV).

Have an articulate adult assume the role of Joshua and read a prepared "charge" such as the following which Joshua may well have given on that occasion.

> Hear, O Israel. The Lord our God is one Lord! We are assembled here today in fulfillment of Moses' commandment to us concerning the remembrance of God's guidance. Remember, O Israel, the night God took the firstborn of Egypt but spared ours. Remember, O Israel, our salvation from the Egyptian army through the touch of God on the Red Sea. Remember, O Israel, the wrath of Moses when he descended from the Mount of God and found our fathers worshiping a god made with their own hands. Remember, O Israel, God's constant provision for us through the daily manna. Remember finally, O Israel, the mistake of our fathers when they saw this land; they thought God too weak to conquer the inhabitants thereof, and only Caleb and I are left from that multitude. This day we have gathered together to remind ourselves of God and His power, for men forget easily and turn to their own affairs and ignore Jehovah our

God. This day God has given His people another chance at gaining their inheritance; let not the worm of doubt infest us as it did our fathers. Let the curses begin!"

Now, starting with the first curse, have the groups alternate the reading of their declarations in unison.

The picnic could well end with a church family sing. Voices blended in praise after a joyful experience can be beautiful. Have the person in charge of music use a variety of songs — rounds, hymns, and old familiar campsite tunes for all ages.

An amateur photographer in your congregation should catch the mood of the day, both humorous and serious, on film. Post the pictures on a bulletin board or other conspicuous location to bring back pleasant memories after the event.

Be sure someone is assigned cleanup. The premises should be left as clean or cleaner than they were when the picnic began.

Promotion of an all-church picnic is essential. Be sure your people know the date and time well in advance so they can plan their family and personal schedules accordingly. I've found it effective to have a competent person in the church make a large sign advertising the picnic. A role of butcher paper can be used. This should be twelve-to-fourteen feet in length and have a catchy phrase in order to get everyone's attention. Post the sign in a conspicuous location. An insert in the midweek and the Sunday bulletins just before the picnic is essential. It should contain the schedule of picnic activities, a map directing church members to the picnic site, the picnic theme, what to bring, exact time, cost if any, transportation information, and so forth. The names and responsibilities of persons assisting with the picnic should be included. The name and phone number of the person in charge should also be listed.

Service Projects

Adults need to be involved in service projects. This is that element of the total program for adults in which they learn to contribute to the welfare of others by performing acts of helpfulness. Service is to be seen as the outcome of Christian worship and education. The life and work of Christ constitutes a foundation for service projects. Adults should bear in mind that through service projects they are projecting Christ by showing and sharing His love. Expressing Christ's love in meaningful and practical ways contributes to one's spiritual growth. Jesus trained the Twelve, and in doing so He stressed that what they learned from Him was to be shared with others.

The love of Christ, the needs of others, and the values to the participants should be kept in mind when planning service projects. This balance should be evident so that the benefits of service projects will be more enduring.

Some service projects may be limited to activities within the church. Other service projects may be designed to help adults beyond the boundaries and buildings of the church. Following are some service projects that can be done within the church: preparing rooms each Sunday for class use, greeting strangers, making name tags, taking the offering, serving as usher, mailing letters, preparing news releases, mailing notices, ordering supplies, playing the piano, picking up hymnals, singing in the choir, painting classrooms, repairing the church structure, performing yard work, and assuming various officer/leader/worker roles in the church.

The projects listed below suggest the wide range of possibilities outside the church:

Involving neighbors in a Bible study
Visiting Sunday school and church prospects
Visiting those in hospitals
Visiting the elderly in their homes
Conducting worship and other services
   in rest homes
Welcoming new community residents
Contacting and praying with the bereaved
Reading to the blind
Transporting children, the elderly,
   or college students to church

Distributing Christian literature

Assisting in community service projects
such as the Meals on Wheels program
for the elderly

Doing errands for shut-ins

Conducting services in jails

Planning and implementing a picnic or
excursion for the underprivileged

Assisting in witnessing campaigns

Sponsoring a coffeehouse or other
outreach center

Building a cabin or other Christian
camp facility

Short-term conference or denominational
projects in the United States or Canada

Short-term projects to assist in mission
efforts abroad

Retreats

Retreats are another legitimate aspect of ministry to adults. Jesus told His disciples, "Now come along to some quiet place by yourselves, and rest for a little while" (Mark 6:31, Phillips). Thus the disciples had to escape the pressures of constant ministering. Today's world presses in on the believer in such a way as to require finding a place of solace. A retreat can be such a place. It is a time to "get away from it all." It is an opportunity to regroup thoughts, emotions, commitments, and goals. It is a time to grow spiritually. A good retreat is like a pebble thrown into a pond. The ripples gradually spread and affect all of the waters.

There are a variety of reasons for conducting retreats: planning, inspiration, ministry development, special projects, communication development, study, motivation, and so forth. In fact, there are as many reasons as there are needs within the church body. Jesus took His disciples out on the boat away from the crowds and pressures for a purpose. A retreat can edify and strengthen the church body just as worship services, Bible studies, and prayer meetings do. Each is different in structure and function, but each has a distinct purpose.

Effective retreat planning begins with the determination of the purpose for the retreat. Once the overall purpose has been decided upon, specific goals can be formulated. The establishing of goals, of course, will determine the programming for the retreat and will aid its leaders in judging its success. Careful attention to the following details will assure a smooth flowing, successful retreat: determine whom the retreat is for, identify the purpose of the retreat, establish goals, appoint a planning committee, reserve facilities, plan the program, gather resources, contact speakers or other participants, create the schedule, develop ground rules, recruit and train leaders, arrange for meals, registration, transportation, and insurance, outline promotion and budget, plan for evaluation.

Following are some kinds of retreats that might be practicable:

A Couples' Overnight Retreat. Every couple periodically needs an overnight retreat to keep their marriage fresh and alive. The one evening plus the next day of a couples' overnight retreat is for couples only, no children. Friday evening plus all day Saturday, at a retreat area or motel, would be most appropriate. The agenda for such a retreat could include spiritual refreshment, reflection, goal setting, romantic pursuits, and recreation. An agenda or suggested schedule of activities involving these elements can be prepared in advance for each couple. Study materials such as a Christian paperback could be included as part of the retreat format.

A Family Retreat. A weekend family retreat might be a good spring or summer activity. Along with activities such as table and outdoor games, crafts, and hikes, you can have times of singing and study. You might order and use some resources designed to promote interaction among family members.

Father/Son and Mother/Daughter Retreats. These are good variations of a family retreat. It is important to strengthen the ties between fathers and sons and between mothers and daughters. The format for such informal retreats could be about the same as a family retreat.

Leadership Retreat. This could be a time to evaluate last year's effectiveness and to establish goals and objectives for the future. Considerable planning could result from this kind of retreat.

Make-a-Film Retreat. The availability of Super 8s has opened the door to creative filmmaking. So use the movie camera to help your group express itself and its ideas. There are many ideas to choose from. ''The Joys of Being a Christian,'' and ''God Speaks Through Our Environment'' are just two suggestions. Have participants write a script, then pick a location and start shooting. Have the film developed and share it with others.

Meditation Retreat. During this weekend retreat, concentrate on learning what it means to meditate. Practice personalizing, visualizing, memorizing, and meditating on Scripture.

Motel Retreat. Why not rent a block of adjoining motel rooms for a retreat? The swimming pool, meeting rooms for study and discussions, and a special restaurant will make the experience worthwhile. Some motels may even offer a reduced rate for such a group.

Twenty-four-Hour Retreat. Devote twenty-four hours to exploring and experiencing a given theme. Have films, games, simulations, speakers, work projects, and anything you can think of, all centered around one basic theme. Saturation is the key. Pick current topics for the best results.

Scripture Retreat. A popular retreat format is the study of a book of the Bible. For a group interested in discovering the Word, this is an excellent way to spend a weekend. Cover the entire book in one weekend. Timothy, James, Philippians, Amos, Jonah, and Ephesians are very popular and contain excellent material. Use the theme of the book you select as your retreat theme.

Camping

Camping is an excellent opportunity for adults to meet

in face-to-face relationships that are genuine. This is enhanced as they live out-of-doors together in a Christian community. Nature has a wholesome, cleansing effect upon our highly pressured lives. Camping is an opportunity for adults to live at a relaxed tempo and to reassess their life values. It also can be a time in which they develop a sense of self-reliance and an appreciation for the skills of others. Adults may discover God as Creator in a fresh way in camp. They may learn more about the wonderful ways in which God provides for them. Through hiking, preparing food, singing, and other group experiences, adults can know and appreciate one another much sooner than they could through any other activity of the church. Camping encourages cooperation and a sense of Christian community. It helps develop a new perspective concerning one's relationship to God, to his fellowman, and to his family.

The most relevant kind of camping for adults is that involving the whole family. Many people believe that time is going very rapidly. Some young people complain about the speed with which their lives are being spent. Another complaint is the lack of time for fellowship with other Christians and even with members of one's own family. Frequently, families do little together that is significant. Even the home has become a place where people eat and sleep but share little fellowship. Most family members do their own thing. Family camping radically changes this. It provides opportunities for fellowship and sharing life even while individual interests are being pursued. Each family member discovers personal joys and the greater joy of being part of the family unit. Roles change when the family goes camping. Mother becomes more than a cook, housekeeper, and family referee. Father is more than one who spends the working day and frequent evenings away as breadwinner. Children find specific duties that require fulfillment if the family well-being is to be preserved.

Family camping programs should include a balance between activities for families as a unit and opportunities for the special interests of adults, children, and youth.

Total fragmentation of the family must be avoided. However, parents will appreciate periods when they can worship and discuss as adults. During adult sessions, daytime activities can occupy younger children, and study/discussions can be planned for youth. Family camping should include both instruction and sharing. Leaders who spend most of their time preaching should be avoided.

Many families may come to camp with no special relationship together in studying the Word. One of the goals of family camp programming should be related to helping bring mother, father, and the children together in Bible study and prayer. This practice established at camp may continue when the family returns home.

Some portion of each day's program should require the family to work together on a project or presentation. An example of this is Patriotism Day. Each family prepares a skit, plans a song or some other form of expression to demonstrate love for country. Every family member must participate. Red, white, and blue are prominent colors in dress and decor, challenging the imagination.

Captivating to both children and adults are various pantomime exercises. A nursery rhyme, Dad's occupation, a moment in history, or a biblical event are some categories that might be selected for an evening's delightful entertainment with every family member involved.

Every family camp should have a purpose. This should be clarified in writing. One that I like is, "To help families discover the distinctives of the Christian home and to make it convenient to experience these while at family camp." Families then could identify the distinctives of the Christian home which are to be experienced at family camp. Then programming should provide opportunities to exercise these Christian family distinctives. Following are some ideas which contribute to such programming:

Family Fun Night. Divide into groups of four to six couples, joined by their children of all ages. Each group meets in an open area to play games. Each father leads one game. Games can be followed by songs and a few skits, possibly by members of the continuing family camp staff. Possibly a film on a family interest can be shown. Close the evening with refreshments.

Vespers. Each family will be responsible for evening vespers at camp. All members of a family can participate, or they can have one or more members represent their family. Involving the children adds great potential for creativity.

Dining at Camp. Families eat together as family units. Any family may start a hymn or chorus with others joining them. Prayer is offered at each table. A father is responsible to pray or ask someone to pray.

"Wives Only" Session. Once a day the ladies need to discuss topics such as "Understanding My Role in the Home," "Personal Devotions for a Busy Mother," "Learning the Art of Listening Love," "Understanding My Children," and "Relating to My Neighbors." During the "Wives Only" sessions, the fathers may spend time with their children. This should involve activities which can be continued after camp such as fishing, playing in the sandbox, doing nature projects, and so forth.

Men's Sessions. Once each day the men will meet to discuss things from their viewpoint such as "Communicating Christ at Work," "Community Activities," "Aiding the Church," "Strengthening My Family," "Little Things Essential to Happiness in Marriage," and "Father/Son and Father/Daughter Activities."

Bible Exploration. Small groups of parents meet for inductive Bible study. Each group should have one couple who is trained in how to lead a discussion group so all participate.

Day Camp. Each morning from nine until noon the children are in day camp.

Afternoon Activities. The entire afternoon is invested in family activities. Several families may enter into the same activity such as swimming, boating, canoeing, hiking, sports, nature recreations, and sight-seeing.

Evening Program. In the evening after the preteen

children are in bed, parents and older teens occasionally meet together for a film, informal singing, sharing, and/or praying around an indoor or outdoor campfire. (A baby patrol needs to be provided to check on small children.)

Would You
1. identify the values of play in a ministry to adults?
2. describe workable devotions for a picnic using the special features of the out-of-doors?
3. name six or more kinds of retreats?
4. indicate the most relevant kind of camping for adults?

Your Move
1. Think of a picnic in which you participated anytime in the past which you enjoyed. List the factors which made it enjoyable.
2. Identify five service projects that can be done within your own local church and five without.
3. Determine the purpose for a father/son retreat and then establish three goals related to that purpose.
4. Name an aspect of family life that is changed radically through family camping.

chapter

5 Special Groups

Can You
1. explain the first step in starting a Christian Growth Group in your church?
2. identify the primary concern of single adults?
3. specify six objectives of an organization for senior adults?
After studying chapter 5 you can.

"Missing last week's session was like missing a meal." With these words, Sue expressed her regret for being unable to enjoy the benefits of her small sharing group. She is among the many who are finding new meaning in their church life through such experiences.

When something ranks as high as a meal, it is important. It is anticipated. Personal schedules are arranged to accommodate it. Other activities are shifted so that it can be included.

Christian Growth Groups

Sue's group is called a Christian Growth Group. Members search for God's direction and help through two means. One is study of the Bible or a Christian book. The other is prayer.

Members learn spiritual truths from studying the group's assigned readings. Sue and the others apply these truths to their lives. Thus biblical principles become real. They are no longer just statements to be identified from Scripture. They mean something. This enables Sue to better live the Christian life.

The group taught Sue to assume responsibility for others. She moved from self-centeredness to other-centeredness. In Luther's terminology, she became a Christ to her brother. As the group developed through time, the outpouring of concern for one another became one of its chief characteristics and one of the major motivations for continuing.

We are commanded to "bear one another's burdens, and so fulfil the law of Christ" (Galatians 6:2, RSV). A Christian Growth Group accomplishes this. It opens members to intimacy — relationships in which persons, free of distrust and hidden motives, meet at the center of their lives, not just at the fringes. From this a freedom emerges which overcomes suspicions and fears. People become close and share. Acceptance is unconditional. And this is extraordinarily beautiful. Frequently it is therapeutic.

Surely many experienced this in John Wesley's "class meetings" to which Christian Growth Groups can be compared. In defense of his class meetings, Wesley wrote: "Many now happily experienced that Christian fellowship of which they had not so much as an idea before. They began to 'bear one another's burdens,' and naturally to 'care for each other.' As they had daily a more intimate acquaintance with, so they had a more endeared affection for, each other."

It is not necessary for a minister to lead all groups. However, Christian Growth Groups should be church centered and controlled. Problems related to forming splinter groups, developing heresies, and dividing the working force are minimized when the church takes the initiative and organizes the groups. Leaders usually can be prepared by the pastor or director of adult ministries through several explanatory sessions. In some groups, leadership may rotate. After groups are functioning, the pastor or director of adult ministries should meet regularly with group leaders to provide coordination and direction.

A group may study the Bible, a paperback which comments on the Bible, or a Christian book which deals with a topic of concern to participants. In addition to study, group activities should include sharing, prayer, fellowship, and outreach. Through these, participants meet each other as partners in a common struggle to grow.

Christian Growth Groups do not replace the need for and value of worship services. Just the opposite occurs. Growth groups enrich and give new meaning to Sunday services. And these services can give new meaning to small group experiences. The worship service is for public proclamation and exposition of the gospel. Attendance at these services prevents small groups from becoming introverted and out of touch with the totality of God's message to the world.

Small group experiences, on the other hand, prevent larger worship services from becoming overly formal, ritualized, impersonal, and sterile. Congregational worship services and Christian Growth Group experiences complement each other. Each provides what the other lacks. Both are needed.

In recent years many churches have found that Christian Growth Groups provide fantastic opportunities for reaching adults and winning them to Christ. Many adults who are unchurched will consider attending a Bible study group in a home long before they will agree to attend a church.

The first step in starting Christian Growth Groups is to explain their purpose and format at a meeting of the whole church constituency such as at a Sunday morning worship service. A poll should then be taken of those interested. See the sample poll on page 63 of this text which includes Christian Growth Groups among other adult ministries activities.

Next the director of this activity enlists host couples, secures teachers, and orders lesson materials under the guidance of the pastor. During this process those who have indicated an interest in Christian Growth Groups are contacted concerning their preferences for meeting times, fellow group members, teachers, and resource materials. They are then personally invited by the director to join the specific group which most closely meets their preferences.

ATTENTION:

FREE METHODIST ADULTS

Supply name and home phone, if you care to.

We need your help! What programs should exist to meet your needs? Our adult ministries staff has been considering this question, and now your advice is requested. Please respond to the following possibilities:

SENIORS

Special activities to provide senior adults opportunities for:

Fellowship and companionship — Consideration of common problems
Bible study and spiritual discussions — Trips and tours
Creative things to do — Service to church and the needy

As a senior adult I personally am _____, am not _____ interested.

MIDWEEK FAMILY NIGHT

Our current all-church prayer service will continue as is. Any additional options would have at least one-fourth of the time spent in prayer. Please check one of the following program options which most interests you:

_____ In-depth Bible study (expository teaching of God's Word structured differently from that of Sunday school)

_____ Christian family-life skills (parenting, communication, roles of family members, husband/wife relationships)

_____ Personal spiritual growth

_____ Person-to-person evangelism

_____ The Christian and contemporary issues

_____ Other (please explain on back)

_____ Interested only in the present format

CHRISTIAN GROWTH GROUPS

Small group direct study of the Bible or indirect study through use of Christian paperbacks — Resources selected by participants — Groups decide to meet weekly or biweekly, also place and time — Church coordinator provides direction and suggestions.

I personally am _____, am not _____ interested.

OTHER ADULT PROGRAMS

If you personally are interested, please give us your ideas about:

A different type of Sunday school class — Weekend retreats
Special activities for adult singles — Seminars on special topics
ACT (leadership and service) courses — All-church fellowship activities
Other possibilities

An alternative would be for the groups' hosts or leaders to invite these persons.

An effective group size is six to twelve persons. Whenever a group gets larger than twelve, part of its membership should break off and form a new group. A Christian Growth Group may meet in a home, church classroom, restaurant, office, factory lounge, or any place providing privacy.

At this point after groups are established, an invitation is given to the entire church constituency to join a Christian Growth Group. This may be in the form of inserts in the midweek and Sunday bulletins. Be sure to include pertinent information concerning each group such as meeting time, location, resource being studied, and phone number of the group's contact person.

Group members should be encouraged to invite their unchurched neighbors, associates, and friends. These new members will not be grounded in the Bible, nor will they come prepared. Consequently, care should be taken to involve them in the session dialogue. For this reason, it is wise not to make in-depth study assignments as preparation for group sessions.

The setting for a Christian Growth Group should be casual. The atmosphere should make those who come feel comfortable. If a group meets in a home, the family room or living room seems the natural choice. However, sometimes groups prefer the dining room where they can have their Bibles before them on a table and where the relationship is a little closer.

As guests arrive, it will be the responsibility of the host to greet them at the door and make them feel welcome and comfortable. If a new person is joining the group, time should be taken for introductions and some casual personal sharing in order to make the newcomer feel at ease. The host should provide extra copies of the Bible or other resource for guests who may arrive without one. As the group begins, everyone should have the resource being studied. If the Bible is being studied directly, a variety of versions is helpful for discussion of various ways in which the passage is stated. This also gives a greater opportunity to the group to interact with one another as they read the various versions.

The major purpose of group sessions is to study Scripture directly or indirectly with a view to personal application through interaction and dialogue. Most Christians have little experience with meaningful dialogue. To aid this, three types of questions should be asked about the biblical passage. What does it say? What does it say to me? What does it say to me for this specific day?

The leader should allow the Bible to speak for itself. Avoid quoting other authorities such as "my pastor says," or "the *Christian Reader* says," or "I read somewhere." Encourage all to take part, but don't put anyone on the spot by calling his name and then asking the question. Ask a question, give all a chance to think, then call on someone who appears to have an answer. After he speaks, say, "What do the rest of you think?"

Note the following hints regarding Christian Growth Groups:

1. Most groups meet weekly for an hour and a half. However, some groups, particularly those meeting in the evening, have a session every other week.

2. Sessions should start promptly and end on time because everyone's schedule is already crowded. This is especially true when participants have baby-sitters with their children during the class session. An effective policy is that refreshments are never served.

3. The person who leads the study learns the most. Periodically changing the leadership prevents the group from getting into a rut. No one should be forced to take a turn leading, but soon most people find they enjoy it. Participation and interest are increased by rotating the leadership each week.

4. Persons learn together. One person's insights sharpen others' understanding of an area, and their thoughts in turn stir further study.

5. It is healthy for a group to have people from various

backgrounds to share ideas and learn together.

6. Stick to the chapter under consideration. Don't jump around in the Bible. Learn everything you can from this chapter or topic.

7. Avoid tangents which frequently become the exchange of mutual ignorance. If tangents come up, say, "Do we find the answer to that problem here?" or "What does this paragraph seem to emphasize?" or "Let's finish the chapter, and then those who want to discuss this question can stay and do so."

8. Christian Growth Group sessions should be encouraged to abandon activity during the months of July and August. This will allow opportunity to regroup when they reorganize in September or October. An intelligent approach would be that no more than 50 percent of those who were in an original group be allowed to join the same group again. This process should be diplomatically promoted as S.O.P. (standard operating procedure).

A form of Christian Growth Group is the Tri-W (Weight, Will, and the Way) program. The main thrust of this is the weekly meeting where women find mutual encouragement for living a victorious, disciplined, and meaningful life. The emphasis includes weight control exercises, nutrition, and systematic personal devotions. Typically, one-hour weekly meetings are scheduled for a ten-week period. Your denominational director of adult ministries or women's organization president should have additional information about Tri-W.

Single Adult Ministry

Many adults in the United States and Canada are single, and the number is growing. About 50 million persons, age eighteen and over, in the United States are single. This computes to approximately one out of three adults. There are about twice as many adult singles today in the United States and Canada as there were a decade ago. They may well be called our largest minority.

Single adults comprise four basic categories: (a) the

temporary single who expects to marry when the circumstances are right; (b) the career single, unmarried as a result of a series of choices or because the right person didn't appear; (c) the widow or widower with or without responsibilities of children; (d) the divorced or separated person with or without children.

A single adult is a unique individual for whom Christ died, one who has the same basic needs, wants, and desires as those of married persons. Such a person is an adult who happens to be single. Luke 2:52 indicates, "Jesus increased in wisdom and stature, and in favor with God and man." He increased mentally (in wisdom). He increased physically (in stature). He increased spiritually (in favor with God). And He increased socially and emotionally (in favor with man). All persons, single or married, have these same developmental task areas. Within these broad areas singles have the following needs:

The Need for Relationships. Loneliness is generally identified as the primary concern of single adults. Often they have no one who is "special" — who really cares about them. Christ can provide an atmosphere so those who are alone are not lonely. You can share things with Christ when He is in your life. And relationships with others in the "family of God" are greatly valued. The regular Saturday night singles fellowship/study group with which I worked for several years frequently continued well into Sunday morning.

The Need to Communicate. Situations are valuable where people open up to each other with no strings attached. "Brother/sister" relationships in groups based on unconditional acceptance are essential. These need to be free from romantic implications or pressures.

The Need for Increased Self-esteem. It's okay to be single. Every person has validity in himself and not just as part of a larger unit. One is a whole number. Each person is a unique, unrepeatable miracle of God.

Overcoming Bias. Society imposes a strong bias or pressure for persons to marry. However, singleness is not a holding pattern for something else. It is not a time for treading water until marriage. God has called every person to live *now.* The challenge is to be His man or woman now in the life situation we have, under His direction. Ultimately, our only true possession is our attitude toward life. We give that to God when we view life as an adventure with Him.

Spiritual Needs. All of us need to develop the richness of the interior self committed to Christ. A widow related that once in a while she feels blue and feels like crying. But she says to herself on those occasions, "I can't cry now because of the children. But just wait until tonight." Then she said, "At night, the Lord puts His loving arms around me, and there just isn't anything to cry about." This is not to imply that one should never cry to God because this may be of value to some. Another person shared with me that he has recently discovered "the complete sufficiency of Christ" in his single situation.

Emotional Needs. Some singles may have deep emotional needs, scars, or hurts. Divorce or the death of a mate can wring the life from a person and leave one alone, afraid, guilty, and on the sidelines. Unless healing and wholeness are brought into life through Christ, such a person can remain permanently scarred and hurt.

Educational Needs. Legal advice may be needed for the newly singled, such as the person recently widowed or divorced. Other singles may have learning needs related to the handling of finances, job reentry, communication skills, assertiveness, or roommates. Some need help in parenting — both instruction and assistance from others.

Sexuality Needs. The Scriptures clearly forbid fornication, adultery, and homosexual practices. God places limits on our sexual behavior but never on the expression of our sexuality. Human sexuality is not just a few particular acts or behaviors; it is what we are, our very essence. It is everything we do and are as God's male or female person. There are many means for enjoying legitimate relationships with members of the opposite sex.

A Positive View of Singleness. In I Corinthians 7:7, Paul

views singleness as a gift from God. Further in that chapter, he explains that the single person can give his undivided devotion to the Lord. By implication, at least, he is suggesting that there are opportunities for Christian service unique to the single. What a positive view of singleness — a gift from God that can be used for His purposes.

The average church is family, couple, youth, and child oriented. Special programs are planned and implemented for them. The same efforts must be expended to meet the needs of singles. This is necessary to conserve them for Christ and develop their spiritual potential. A conscious sensitivity to the singles in your church is the necessary first step.

Any ministry to adult singles should not completely segregate them. They need the specialized activities of a separate singles program to help them find fellowship and develop maturity within the particular circumstances of their lives. However, they also need to be integrated as a welcome part of the full church family. There need to be opportunities for singles to be involved with couples and families both in church-sponsored and private activities.

Some churches use cluster family activities in connection with family month, family night during the summer, or as part of an evening vacation Bible school. This is a group of twelve to fifteen persons including one or more nuclear (biological) families, single adults, senior adults, and children or youth whose parents are not active in church. Relational and worship experiences requiring personal interaction are done as a cluster group.

Christian Growth Groups comprising adult singles, couples, and youth can provide an excellent setting for sharing, Bible study, prayer, and personal growth to occur. Church leaders can encourage this kind of in-depth relating where persons of various backgrounds and circumstances minister to each other. Such a group can be one's surrogate family.

Sunday school classes exclusively for singles should be provided for those of college and career (or Agape

Fellowship) age. Older singles may want to be integrated into classes with other adults.

One church rapidly raised its consciousness regarding single adults by having an articulate person speak from experience on "being a Christian single."

Social events such as an all-church picnic or potluck dinner should involve singles. Such events should be promoted as *total* church affairs for everyone, regardless of age, sex, marital status, membership, or attendance record. These are opportunities to promote the sense and benefits of being a member of a "church family."

Sunday fellowship after the morning worship service can bring positive results to singles. Coffee and doughnuts provide the setting where singles meet visitors, discuss the sermon, and keep up with current happenings.

Churches can organize procedures whereby singles are invited to the homes of effective, loving families. Then, singles should be encouraged to entertain in return.

Sunday school class activities and parties need to avoid becoming couples oriented. Singles should share leadership roles in planning such events.

Care for widows is a responsibility of the church (see I Timothy 5 and Acts 6). Several years ago my church was paid a fine compliment when a mother and her three sons moved back some eighty miles into our area upon the death of the husband and father. The move was made so they could resume their previous involvement in the church. I remember very well those discussions in our church's governing body as we considered our individual responsibilities to this widow and her sons.

A separate organization may be the best means for providing specialized activities to singles. Most denominations have adopted this means for children and youth and to a lesser extent for couples (Marriage Enrichment and Marriage Encounter). A wide range of activities can be sponsored by a singles organization. Smaller churches may join with others in sponsoring such an organization.

Following are steps for organizing and implementing a special ministry to single adults:

Inventory. Take inventory of the single adults in your church. This might be done through placing a card in the church bulletin or having a portion of it which can be torn off. Singles would be requested on this to indicate their name, age category, and the basis of their singleness, that is, never married, divorced, separated, widow, or widower. The results of this inventory would need to be checked with people knowledgeable about the church membership, such as the pastor or Board of Christian Education, to be certain no one is missed.

Exploratory Meeting. All of the adult singles in the church family could be invited to an exploratory meeting where the idea of a ministry to adult singles is discussed. Before the meeting, they should be informed that the possibility of a separate organization for adult singles will be explored.

As an alternative it may be preferable to have a group of twelve or fourteen represent the singles in the church. This group might well be called the "dream team." The reason for this alternative might be that there are too many singles for all to attend such a meeting. Another reason might be that the specialness of being asked would assure a more productive group. If a "dream team" is used, be certain it represents all ages and bases of singleness.

Identify Needs. Don't assume you know the needs of adult singles. Ask them. Be supportive, open, and encouraging as needs are expressed. List them on the chalkboard for all to see as they are identified. Singles will respond to the request to identify their needs.

Meeting Needs. Discuss what can be done to meet needs. Is there something the church can do to meet needs? Would an organization help to meet needs?

Identify Leaders. Whom shall we ask to assume responsibility for activities, projects, or programs to meet needs? Ask singles for their help in assuming leadership. Ask for help regarding ideas as to who would be a good leader. Remember that positive people attract others. Positive, happy people help persons who hurt. So, get positive people as leaders. Someone, either an adult single or a couple, should be identified who will assume responsibility on a continuing basis for a ministry to adult singles. This leader must perceive this as a personal ministry. The leader(s) must assume an ongoing responsibility for being there, for counseling, for introducing new members, and for providing continuity in an organization where members frequently come and go. This cohesive factor is sorely needed. The person(s) performing this role *must work with singles* rather than tell them what to do.

Conduct Activities. Carry out activities that allow for personal growth on the part of singles. Be sure activities are designed to meet the needs which have been identified.

Don't expect to be perfect as you begin the organization. Plan to learn and be responsive to the verbal wishes and the nonverbal messages regarding the program. Convey an attitude of experimentation to the members so they realize the program or ministry will grow and is responsive to their wishes.

The vast majority of singles *are* leading meaningful, productive lives. The church's task is to help in this process. Its leaders should constantly affirm singles. Don't be a matchmaker. Don't imply in speech or prayer that the norm is to be married. It may not be for many in your church.

Senior Adult Ministry

"As we grow older, we tend to become more of what we really are," a wise elder recognized. Aging is a continuous process from birth to death. The Bible has some beautiful pictures of the older person who lives the life of faith. Yet, the Bible also pictures the problems and trials of the latter years as "evil days" and years in which one has no pleasure because of physical deterioration. Approximately one in eight persons in the United States and Canada is in the senior adult category, that is, age sixty-one and older. And this proportion is growing.

Who is concerned about the elderly? The older

generation is largely ignored by growth-minded congregations. Yet elderly men and women may soon become the fastest growing age-group. Some leaders have suggested that the church of the future is the one with the program for senior adults.

Senior adults have the following problems or difficulties:

Income. Approximately 25 percent of senior adults live below the "poverty" line. As the cost of living rises, social security benefits seldom keep up. Furthermore, women, because they usually outlive men, form the biggest portion of the elderly and suffer the most.

Health. Health problems and concerns increase in direct proportion to one's age.

Transportation. Public transportation is often expensive and inconvenient. Suspension of driver's licenses at arbitrary age limits contributes to the problem. Likewise, spiraling insurance rates for the elderly add to this concern.

Public Attitude. Old people frequently are shunted aside. Many elderly live in rural areas or older communities from which youth have fled. Many elderly live in cities where uncaring neighbors and fear of robbery reinforce loneliness.

Self-attitude. A diminished self-image is the result of alienation and isolation. Frequently, they feel they have nothing to contribute, since they think they are unwanted. They need to be needed. And in fact they are more needed than they or the public recognize. They have learned much which, if heeded, will avoid many mistakes by younger persons.

Loneliness. The elderly long for relationships with others and friends with whom they can relate at a deep level. The loss of a mate and often the loss of their friends, in later years, add to the need for companionship.

Nutrition. Typically limited income and new physiological needs created by aging require special foods.

Lessening of Abilities. Frequently, decreasing ability to move about, to see, to think clearly, or to hear becomes exaggerated in the perceptions of the elderly.

Do you ever wonder what you can do for the senior citizens of your church, or, conversely, what they can do for you? Perhaps the most important impact the church can make on the lives of older persons is to let them know that they are important. Let them know they are important to Christ, important to the congregation, and important to the community in which they live. If you do not already have some sort of concrete program for this segment of your congregation, hasten to remedy the situation.

A ministry for senior adults in the local church should provide opportunity for (1) fellowship and companionship, (2) fun, (3) creative things to do, (4) worship and prayer, (5) Bible study and discussions beyond Sunday services, (6) service to church and the needy, (7) assuming responsibility, (8) discussion of common problems, (9) freedom from competition with younger persons, (10) planning by themselves, and (11) recognition as being important in the total church's program.

What can a local church do to provide these opportunities and meet the needs of the elderly? A senior adult program must recognize the vast talent reservoir among seniors. With a little nudging, the church can secure the services of a great many retirees whose knowledge and skills are greatly needed and ought to be used. The former secretary can engage in dictation, typing, manuscript and other filing, mimeographing, and so forth. Use former painters and interior decorators to improve the church building. A retired journalist can write for the church paper and prepare church histories. A retired camera buff can record on film much that is of significance to the church. Plumbers, electricians, surveyors, and accountants can be used in the church doing tasks for which they are trained. Visitation ministries, telephone reassurance ministries, camp dining room hostesses, gift shop workers, camp office workers, short-term missionaries, a grandfather for the nursery department, an adopted grandfather for children who have none or whose real grandfather is many miles away — all of these can be avenues of service by the elderly.

A separate organization may well be necessary in order to make your ministry to senior adults fully effective in meeting their needs. If you should want to organize, the procedures outlined on page 71 to 72 of this book for organizing single adults are applicable. Please refer to them.

Although it is desirable for a group to have officers, be careful not to elect people too quickly. Give the group a chance to jell first. Small groups may function only with a president, vice-president, secretary/treasurer, and program chairman. Involve as many as possible. Every senior adult should have the opportunity to serve on a committee. In fact, all activities may be carried out through committees rather than by elected offices. Some may be standing committees, and others are ad hoc (appointed for particular occasions). Committees might include program, entertainment, refreshments, arrangements, invitations, decorations, telephone, and visitation.

Encourage the group to select a creative name, a name like the following: Golden Age Club, Golden Years Club, Evergreen Club, XYZ Club (Xtra Years of Zest), Golden Harvesters, Seasoned Soldiers, Live Long and Like It Club, Young in Heart, Keen-Agers, SALT (Senior Adults Living Triumphantly), SAIL (Senior Adults Inspired Living), Voyagers, Golden Circle Club, Modern Maturity Fellowship, Elder Blooms, Sage Agers, Upper Crust, Diamond Set, or Post Graduates.

You may want to identify objectives for a seniors organization. These are guidelines for activities. Any activity would be designed to achieve one or more of the objectives. Following are objectives adopted by one seniors organization:

Spiritual Growth — Persons can and must grow in a love relationship to Christ throughout their whole lives.

Fellowship — Structured opportunities to overcome loneliness are valuable.

Fun — A good time in Christ is healthful and helpful.

Outreach — People in their eighties can be and have

been won to Christ.

Service — All should serve the body. What's done for Christ and in His name will last.

Education — There are many topics about which seniors need to know more and want to know more.

The following are programming ideas that can be used to assist in achieving objectives:

Talent Program — Music, original poetry, readings, skits, stories. Have an impartial judge, but don't take the results seriously.

Tours and trips to factories, state or provincial capitol or county courthouse, and other points of interest by motorcade or chartered bus.

Luncheons and dinners — Picnics, progressive meals, (one course at each house or section of the church fellowship area and then move on), backward supper for April Fool's Day, meals on a mission theme, or meals which carry out the motif of a well-known church event.

Sharing hobbies and learning new crafts (perhaps an annual hobby show).

Movies on a topic of particular interest to seniors.

A baby show which displays baby pictures of the seniors.

A historical afternoon where tales of childhood are told.

A recording party where cassette tapes are made to be sent to children on Mother's Day or Father's Day.

Travelogues (slides, pictures, or films of one's travels).

Party with a theme such as "Down on the Farm," "Back to School," or "Saint Patrick's Day."

Table games such as dominoes, checkers, Scrabble, and Aggravation.

Group games including spelling matches, croquet, boccie, or Jarts.

Trips to a concert, professional athletic event.

Show and Tell — Bring a valuable personal possession and explain its significance.

Secret Pals

Candlelight supper

Favorite poem or prose

Puppet show

Backyard cookout

Come-as-you-are party

Bible quiz.

Fishing trips

Gag Gift — Have a grab bag of gag gifts and tell how you will use the one you received.

Folk songs, motion songs, barbershop quartets, old-time songs, singspirations

Dramatic presentations by seniors

A presentation by a guest artist of a new craft

Speakers on travels, hobbies, gardening, wood carving, police protection, Social Security, Medicare, legal advice to seniors, community services, emergency medical service, fire protection, and other topics of interest to seniors

Service opportunities might include: helping with church mailings, making or repairing furniture for the children's department of the church, telling stories for children's groups, clipping or collecting news items for the church history or vacation Bible school, collecting materials for the pastor, cleaning house and preparing a hot meal for a shut-in, repairing church hymnals or altar furniture and accessories, building a church bulletin board, visiting new people and shut-ins, or visiting nursing homes as a group for conversation and worship.

Another service opportunity could be "Ring-a-Friend" project. Have senior adults sign up to call a certain number of folks and elderly shut-ins each day at a certain time. A retirement seminar could be held in the local church. Use specialists as consultants. Use older persons themselves to speak from firsthand experience on assigned topics. Emphasize retiring with enjoyment.

In your congregation, you may want to observe a Sunday on aging. Designate a Sunday as a special occasion to highlight the needs and potentialities of older persons within your congregation and the larger community. This might include a special order of service, an appropriate sermon on "Overcoming Age Fright," "Accept Your Age," or "The Best Is Yet to Come." Special discussion programs may occur in adult classes. A fellowship luncheon for all members of the congregation may well occur.

A senior day-care center might be appropriate for larger churches. This could be a portion of the church annex, a storefront, or other location where seniors in the community can be cared for during the day such as is done in children's day-care centers. Another form of this would be a center open to the public for seniors who would drop in and out during the day for fellowship and recreation. Spiritual experiences and evangelism could soon be a part of such a center.

Senior organizations should sponsor worship and Bible study experiences for their members. Prayer groups and Christian Growth Groups can be very effective in contributing to the lives of seniors. See pages 60 to 66 of this book concerning Christian Growth Groups.

Would You
1. explain the first step in starting a Christian Growth Group in your church?
2. identify the primary concern of single adults?
3. specify six objectives of an organization for senior adults?

Your Move
1. Identify the responsibilities of the host for a Christian Growth Group.
2. List three questions a Christian Growth Group leader should ask about a biblical passage.
3. Name the four basic categories of single adults.
4. List numerous service opportunities suggested for seniors organizations which would be appropriate for your church.

Leadership Development

Can You
1. name four critical considerations relating to leadership development?
2. list five or more personal motives a prospect might have for accepting a leadership position in the church?
3. indicate the preferred method for preparing leaders?

After studying chapter 6 you can.

Two shoe salesmen were sent to an impoverished African nation. They arrived in advance of their shoe shipments which were scheduled to follow. Upon looking at the conditions, the first salesman wired back with the statement, "Cancel my shipment. No one here *wears* shoes." The second salesman wired saying, "Triple my shipment. No one here *has* shoes." What a difference in attitude is reflected in these responses to the same conditions. A positive can-do attitude is essential in the person responsible for leadership development in the local church.

A concern for leadership must exist if Christian education is to fulfill its task and provide spiritual renewal and nurture. *Programs* do not provide spiritual nurture; *people* do. People change people. Cultivating leaders is a major function of the church through Christian education. In some denominations the director of adult ministries is responsible for leadership development for all levels of Christian education — children, youth, and adults. In other denominations he may have responsibility only for training leaders of adult groups. Either way, attention needs to be given to leadership development. In *Better Leaders for Your Church,* Weldon Crossland says, "Four indispensables are to be found in every successful church. They are program, organization, morale, and leadership; but the greatest of these is leadership." All responsible officers/workers/leaders are interested in training and development. They have a desire to be successful as measured by God's standards. They realize that success is not measured solely by what we are. It is measured by what we are compared to what we could be. Success is not measured by what we do. It is measured by what we do compared to what we could be doing. With this guide, they seek training not only for themselves but also for others.

Training and leadership development will help the Christian education worker or interested person:

1. Do his or her best to present himself to God as one approved. II Timothy 2:15
2. Become a workman who has no need to be ashamed. II Timothy 2:15
3. Rightly handle the Word of truth. II Timothy 2:15
4. Progress toward becoming the faithful person who will be able to teach others. II Timothy 2:2
5. Effectively teach persons to obey everything Christ commanded. Matthew 28:20
6. Witness in *his* or *her* Jerusalem, Judea, Samaria, and unto the uttermost part of the earth. Acts 1:8

Other reasons for training are:

1. "Leadership training, from the New Testament church until today, has been a chief secret of growing churches" (Win Arn in *How to Grow a Church*).
2. When the church asks a person to accept an assignment, it must also provide training opportunities.
3. Training helps persons to grow: to gain new insights, to obtain new information, and to see new possibilities. Growing leaders are likely to affect growth in others.

There are four critical considerations relating to leadership. These are (1) the person who gets leaders, (2) getting leaders, (3) training leaders, (4) keeping leaders.

The Person Who Gets Leaders

The person who gets leaders must be a model for others, one who exhibits the qualities needed in leaders.

In addition, this person needs to be enthusiastic about the role of Christian education in the church. Enthusiasm is caught from others. The spiritual nurture of individuals and the efficacy of the gospel is something to be enthusiastic about. The person who gets leaders must have self-knowledge. Such a person needs to know his or her strengths and weaknesses. Strong areas must be developed. But work must occur on weaknesses as well. Problem areas in personality must be identified and worked on. These persons must realize that mistakes or defeats need not stop them. They can be stepping-stones to a more effective ministry.

The person who gets leaders needs to constantly work on understanding others' opinions and positions. Such a person must listen and respond to others. He or she knows that leadership is the activity of influencing and directing people toward some goal and directing their cooperation in achieving that goal.

The person who obtains leaders has the following personal traits: humility, a servant heart, a sensitive spirit, an insistence on excellence, initiative, creativity, single-mindedness, empathy, faith in people, the ability to be led, high energy level, adaptability, diplomacy, people-centeredness, fairness, openness, ability to organize, ability to delegate, skill in coordinating events, ability to motivate others, communication skills, human relation skills, and problem-solving skills.

Getting Leaders

Sometimes the following are given as reasons for selecting leaders: "She has plenty of time; let's name her." Or, "His is the first name that comes to mind." Or, "She's not doing anything else in the church." Or, "Let's get him so that he'll become interested in the church!" Or, "You know she just might take it, let's try her." Or, finally, "He's not here to defend himself; let's nominate him." All of these are the wrong reasons. Other persons who should not be chosen for leadership roles are those who are usually against whatever is proposed, those who have a reputation for promising but not performing, those who do not take responsibilities seriously, and those who are already carrying a full load of responsibility in the church.

The following are general characteristics of those to name to leadership positions. The person who: is a good Christian and who owns Christ as his example and Saviour; is a church member and is loyal to the church; has a good mind and a strong, appealing personality; likes people and is in turn liked by them; has a good reputation and Christian walk in the community; is willing to take instruction in leadership training; has a native ability for the position being filled; has interest in the phase of the work under consideration; does well in whatever is undertaken; is conscientious and will follow through; is resourceful; has skills and experience in the particular area of church work under consideration.

Some churches use a talent and interest inventory, taken during a Sunday morning worship service. Persons present indicate their talents and interests on a question-naire form. This form contains the various kinds of tasks, offices, and leadership roles in the church. Results are then tallied and the responses form a pool from which leaders are chosen.

How can prospective leaders understand the signifi-cance of a potential leadership role? How do persons become interested in serving? The following factors contribute to serious consideration of a church leadership position:

Previous Experience in Leadership Roles. Experience teaches that those most willing to serve are those who have assumed responsibility before. Thus persons in their teens should be given responsibility in the church appropriate to their years.

Nothing Succeeds like Success. Persons are willing to share in enterprises that are alive, that are going concerns, that are moving, and that have high morale.

Significance of the Task. Persons must be led to see that a leadership role is a significant thing. They must see that they will be contributing to improving the world's present moral and spiritual condition. For them it will be fulfilling the Great Commission. They will be aiding the achievement of Christ's kingdom.

Understanding the Task. Potential leaders need to understand what the task will be. Possibly a job analysis or a job description would help. The essentials of this are a written description of the job and its relationship to other church positions plus a list of responsibilities. Potential leaders need to know the larger unit of which they are a part. They'll want to know how their role fits into the total church program.

Satisfaction and Pleasure. The potential leader needs to know that what he does will be satisfying. He must know that the best conditions possible for his work will be provided. His initial experiences in a new position should be satisfying.

Fruits of Their Efforts. Potential leaders need to see the results of their work. They need to be motivated to see the potential good through their efforts.

Ample Time. Effective leaders should be given sufficient time to make a decision after being asked to serve. Some may prefer to try out a position before agreeing to accept it permanently.

Official Status. Potential leaders need to know the title and/or official position of the role they're being asked to assume. They need to understand that the position is appointed or elected by official agencies of the church. This lends dignity to the position and constitutes a challenge for achievement.

After analyzing the positions needing to be filled and the available personnel, the responsible person or committee prayerfully and carefully chooses the right person for the right position. The total needs of the church and the most efficient use of human resources enter into these considerations.

There is a variety of ways to offer invitations to persons identified for leadership roles. However, one of the most effective methods is to recruit on a one-to-one basis or by a team of two persons who contact the prospective leader. Adequate time in the prospect's home is typically the best. A phone call or a quick conference on the way to or from a worship service is the least effective approach. Following are some guidelines to help enlist leaders:

1. Be warm and open.
2. Share the church's criteria for the selection of leaders. Indicate how long the person is expected to serve.
3. Inform the prospect with whom he or she will be working and explain working relationships.
4. Provide an opportunity for the prospect to express his or her feelings, hopes, concerns, and personal needs and to ask questions. Explain how skills already developed can be used and assure the prospect that special training is available if needed.
5. Explain the curriculum resources and materials. Provide samples if possible.
6. Don't invite either a yes or no during your initial contact. Let the person think and pray about it for a while. Decide together the length of time that will take and indicate you will make contact again at that time.
7. In your overall efforts, persevere; but do not pressure.

Consider the following personal motives related to accepting a proposed leadership position. Appeal to one or more of these motives, as appropriate.

1. A strong sense of Christian duty
2. A desire to render service to the church
3. A genuine interest and liking for people
4. The conviction that the task needs to be done

5. Consciousness that he possesses the special skills for a given work
6. Loyalty to Jesus Christ
7. The request of a close friend
8. The desire to share
9. An opportunity to influence Christian character
10. The love of children, youth, or adults
11. A vehicle in which to grow spiritually and socially

Think through the step-by-step progression of your oral request to a prospect. Your outline should unfold logically and smoothly. It should move steadily toward the moment of favorable decision. Your presentation should not be diverted from its main purpose. It should follow this order: introduction of the subject, a clear statement of the task, the great importance of the work, the membership of the group to be led, the present activities of the group, the specific duties of the leader, the valid reasons your prospect was chosen from the entire membership of the church, the satisfaction and joy that will flow from doing a job well, and assurance that God's will was sought concerning the right person for the task.

Following the initial presentation, you will be open to answering questions the prospect may have. Always accent the affirmative. See that the conversation moves on levels of substantial agreement and interest. Fervently pray that God will be with you, will guide you, and will give you success. Throughout, exalt the privilege of Christian service. Never say, "This will not take very much of your time." Magnify the task and emphasize that being asked is evidence of confidence and faith in the prospect's abilities. Never argue. Answer fully and frankly all questions that may be asked. Avoid letting your prospect say no except for the most urgent and valid reasons.

Training Leaders

Training leaders is an ongoing process. It should begin during the enlistment interview. You should be suggesting resources for study before the leader begins. Your denominational leadership and service training program should be followed in the training of Christian education leaders. Resources are carefully selected or specially written to be consistent with the denomination's organizational pattern, doctrinal distinctives, and educational approaches.

Denominational leadership and service training programs have a series of awards. Typically, these include a progress card which is awarded for completion of a single course. Then certificates may be awarded for completion of the required courses necessary to prepare one for a specific position in the church. Denominational programs have several levels of certification such as qualified, certified, and master leader designations. Procedures, standards, and other information regarding such programs are usually available in written form. For this information, contact your denominational director of adult ministries.

Learning experiences may occur in organized classes or in the individual study format. The denominational program, regardless of the learning structure, is the preferred method for preparing leaders. The following are some methods that may be used to supplement that program:

Apprentices. The new leader should be assigned as an apprentice to a more experienced leader in the same or similar area. The inexperienced person can have conferences and opportunities to discuss tasks and activities and role performance with the experienced leader.

Supervision. This term indicates personal guidance on the job. It is a plan whereby an experienced leader counsels with and makes suggestions to a less experienced teacher or leader as they work together on problems. The supervisor is not in an authoritative position to the leader. He is considered on a staff or equal relationship. The supervisor helps the new leader acquire greater skill at the points where it is most needed. The supervisor observes the leader or teacher at work and helps recognize strong and weak features of his or her procedures. The supervisor may give an evaluation of a meeting or class. This person offers suggestions for improvement and directs the leader or teacher to helpful resources.

Observation. Opportunities should be provided for leaders to observe successful practitioners in action. Some of these may be in public schools, and some may be persons within the church. Careful plans should be made so that each person may observe the phases of work which are of the most concern. Each observer should know what he or she wants to look for. Just looking around may not be fruitful. Arrangements should be made ahead of time for a conference following the observation. This will provide opportunity for interpretations, explanations, and evaluations.

Guided Reading. There is a widespread and growing interest in church libraries. A good church library may have articles and books relating to effective methods in carrying out various leadership or teaching roles.

Visits from a Specialist. A professional or semi-professional specialist may visit a church and provide suggestions for improving the leadership performance. The conference following the visit may identify several things which will improve the situation.

Church Visiting. Visits to observe effective leaders in other churches may be a source of new ideas, motivation, and inspiration.

Christian Education Seminars and Workers' Conferences. These are meetings in which church workers confer with one another, have opportunity for fellowship, gain valuable information, develop their skills, become motivated, share in planning their work, and see role models of excellent leaders in action. Denominational age level and Christian education executives frequently conduct these events. Opportunities should not be missed to meet and confer with such leaders.

Tutors. A leader may be assigned a tutor who is an experienced person in the leader's task area. This person would periodically meet with and evaluate the leader's work.

Coaching. At intervals, an experienced person may help

leaders with problems. This person provides help in a specific area needing correction.

Keeping Leaders

Once leaders are appointed and trained, the problem becomes to keep them. Typically, leaders accept the task with high hopes and expectations. Later, they may discover that nobody really cares, not even the person who did the original recruiting. They may feel all alone in their task. This is a disillusioning experience. A way to avoid this disillusionment is to support leaders. A support program says we care about you and what you do. This support should be from the total congregation, not just the person recruiting leaders. A supportive climate helps to release power and energy for work. A support program may vary from church to church and within a church from year to year. A variety of ways to offer support should be used. The following are some support strategies that are effective.

Orientation of Leaders. An orientation session or retreat for leaders is very effective at the beginning of their service. This will provide them ways to know the avenues available for carrying out their responsibilities. New leaders have an opportunity through an orientation to understand more fully what is expected of them. Orientation sessions provide an opportunity to explain the "housekeeping matters" involved in the position. These include procedures for securing supplies and resources, for paying bills, and for setting meeting times of boards and committees. Special regulations of the church are also explained at orientation sessions. Sessions should include times for giving out information, for sharing, for fellowship, and for boards, committees, and educational leaders to become acquainted.

Leadership Appreciation Day. Some churches have an annual celebration to feature the importance of leaders and workers in the church. The celebration during this day could include a sermon on preparation for assuming church responsibilities. It also could include a report from the person responsible for leadership education as to specific accomplishments for the year and plans for the future. All church leaders might sit as a body and be recognized some way during this day. Certificates of appreciation and/or an appreciation dinner may be provided.

Dedication and Installation Service. A service of dedication and installation for leaders, if conducted impressively, can be effective in emphasizing the significance of their tasks. A reception could follow the service. In such an informal setting, individual church members can get to know the leaders and express appreciation to them.

Leadership Education Sunday. Those persons who have completed the formalized leadership program of your denomination should be recognized publicly. This will reinforce the significance your church places upon the denominational leadership program. Awards such as progress cards and certificates can be given during this Sunday.

Resources. Resources supported by an adequate budget should be provided for church leaders. Funds should be sufficient for obtaining sufficient printed resources, films, pictures, facilities, and equipment. Help your leaders get these resources.

Learning Opportunities. Most people like to know that they are improving their skills. One of the best means of supporting leaders is to provide opportunities for their further training.

Staff Meetings. These are excellent times for sharing, training, motivating, encouraging, and praying together. Use such meetings (along with other strategies and ideas in this chapter) to assure your leaders that they are not "alone out there."

Criteria for Performance. Don't impose your standards on leaders. Help leaders to look at what really matters in their leadership roles. Help them identify what will determine their success. Perhaps they should identify specific objectives for the quarter or year. Encourage leaders then to evaluate their performance against these criteria.

An Atmosphere with Freedom to Function. Such an atmosphere says to the leader that the congregation trusts him. Persons work better when they feel they are helping to make the decisions which affect them.

Offer Feedback. Provide feedback rather than criticism. Criticism is often one's personal opinion of how something should be done. Feedback is the supplying of data without making a judgment. It describes what was seen and heard and what the effect was. Feedback is given on what is observable, not on hearsay. It is best given when requested or when the person giving it has asked permission to give it.

Practicing the following support ideas will also help to keep leaders:

1. Occasionally publish the names of church leaders.
2. Provide opportunity for continued spiritual growth of your leaders. A deepened, enriched spiritual life offers the best hope for high morale.
3. Keep communication lines open.
4. Plant ideas casually and diplomatically. Frame your ideas in questions and subtle suggestions.
5. Ask advice; show your own need.
6. Do things for your colleagues that make them feel important, not dependent.
7. Neither expect nor want the credit. Give credit to others.
8. Concede unimportant matters and keep the door open to get across what is more important to you and the work.
9. Purposefully let others outshine you, a secret of good leadership if one is big enough to use it.
10. Actually take pride in the achievement of other leaders.
11. Don't hassle leaders with unnecessary meetings and fruitless tasks.
12. Leaders who teach should be given definite times off during the year.

When these support strategies and ideas are carried out within the context of a desire to minister in Christ's name and for His kingdom, positive effects are the result.

Would You
1. name the four critical considerations relating to leadership development?
2. list five or more personal motives a prospect might have for accepting a leadership position in the church?
3. indicate the preferred method for preparing leaders?

Your Move
1. Cite reasoning or data to support the quotation from Weldon Crossland on page 80 concerning the priority of leadership.
2. Place in rank order the factors that contribute to serious consideration of a church leadership position. (See pages 82 and 83.) Put the most important factor first, second most important next, and so on.
3. List three methods for preparing leaders (other than your denomination's leadership and service training program) that would be the most valuable for you.
4. One of the support ideas useful in keeping leaders is to "do things for your colleagues that make them feel important, not dependent." Illustrate two actions that would make them feel important and two that would make them feel dependent.

Leader's Guide

Introduction

Thank you for serving as a trainer of persons interested in ministering in adult Christian education. As leader of the group-learning sessions for this volume, you should seek to radiate to those in training the joy and enthusiasm you have discovered in Christian service. Also, you should approach each session thoroughly prepared and prayerful that God will make the learning time profitable to all. No doubt you will find the following group study suggestions helpful and perhaps stimulating. But be sure to adapt them to the needs of your group and to use your own creative ideas. At times you may wish to review with your class the self-study "Would You?" and "Your Move" sections which accompany each chapter.

Session One
The Foundation of Ministry

Divide your class into small groups of four to six persons. Have each group develop a rank order of significance of the building blocks in the foundation of an expanded ministry to adults. List from the most important to the least important.

Brainstorm as a class (identify without comment) additional building blocks in the foundation of an expanded ministry to adults. List these on the chalkboard. Then allow discussion of each.

Ask class members to individually complete the sentence, The following are the five most pressing needs of persons in my age category. Share responses first in triads (groups of three) and then as an entire class.

Page 11 lists some milestones or discriminating events in the adult life cycle. In groups of three, identify the attitude or emotion (or both) associated with each. Then have these groups identify and discuss other milestones which are not listed.

Dale Carnegie says that in order to *be* enthusiastic you must *act* enthusiastic. Have two persons role-play a Sunday morning announcement to the church concerning a forthcoming all-church picnic. One will illustrate enthusiasm, and the other the lack of it. Then have another two people make such contrasting announcements. Then two more, and so on through the entire class.

Session Two
Marriage and Family Enrichment

Call attention of your class to the four items under "Your Move" at the end of chapter 2. As a group and as appropriate, lead your class in completing each item.

One paragraph on page 22 contains these sentences. "The family is the church in miniature." "The human personality is exposed in the home as nowhere else." "The family can be called the basic unit of Christian education." Lead your class in a guided discussion of each sentence in turn. Emphasize understanding and implications for a local church's expanded ministry to adults.

Select four persons to role-play a family scene and/or discussion which results from the neighbor's dog destroying all six tomato plants in the family garden. Model as many as possible of the insights and suggestions for effective family life contained under the section entitled "Emphasize Family Devotions." Assign roles as follows: George, father; Mildred, mother; Ann, daughter, age 7; Ralph, son, age 10. Allow role-players adequate time to prepare. After the activity, involve all class members in a discussion of what they observed. Ask nonplayers, What would you have done differently? Do you agree with the way George, Mildred, Ann, Ralph acted?

Note item number 7 on page 25 which is a way to get families started in family worship. Have each class member plan the devotions he would conduct in the situation described there. Share and discuss these plans with others in the class.

Session Three
Nurture and Outreach

List on the chalkboard the fifteen nurture and outreach strategies which comprise the topical headings of chapter 3. In small groups of three or four, identify the five most appropriate strategies for your church. Outline how each of the five could be implemented. Have each group share its conclusions with the entire class.

Divide your class into four groups and make one assignment to each: drama, choral speaking, athletics, or puppetry. Each group is to identify three or more objectives for the nurture and outreach strategy it has been assigned. Share findings with the entire class.

In groups of three, plan a program for institutionalized persons. Identify the type of institutionalization first and then the needs of the persons involved. Be sure the program meets needs. Include an outline of the content of all oral presentations planned as part of the program. List titles of songs and scriptural sources used in the program. Share programs with the entire class. Discuss.

As a class using the brainstorming technique, identify a list of six or more current social concerns. Then democratically choose one to consider at length. Lead a guided group discussion of that concern dealing with its dimensions and implications. Next have each person prepare a position paper (several sentences or paragraphs) stating what he believes should be the official position regarding that issue. Each person then will decide what appropriate action should be taken relating to the issue. Share and discuss.

Invite one or more persons to explain to your class the benefits of scriptural memorization. Go outside the class for such person(s) if necessary.

Session Four
Supportive Activities

Be sure your class understands the definition of supportive activities. Ask, How can the objectives of discipleship, nurture, and evangelism be achieved through supportive activities? Divide your class into triads (groups of three) and assign them to discuss the above. Suggest that they think of illustrations in their answer. In each triad, have the person with the most recent birthday report to the entire class.

Assign a different person to lead the class in each of the two fellowship/recreational activities on page 49. Assistance may be needed in understanding these activities and in organizing the class to do them. Commission all class members to assist in this. Continue with each activity only as long as necessary for class members to understand and appreciate it.

Let your class members engage in the picnic devotions as explained beginning on page 50. Pick someone to be Joshua. Divide the rest of the class into Mount Gerizim and Mount Ebal groups. Have each mark the appropriate verses in their Bibles (KJV). Begin the devotions with Joshua speaking from the center of the classroom and the two groups at the sides of the classroom.

Have each class member prepare the words to go on an all-church picnic promotional sign of the type discussed on page 51. Have each person share with the entire class.

Beginning on page 51, service projects, both within and outside the church, are discussed. Lead your class in identifying and discussing additional ones. Write these on the chalkboard under the proper category. Then have each class member separately rank all projects from most significant to least significant in terms of (a) showing and sharing Christ's love and (b) contributing to the spiritual growth of the one doing the service.

Form class members into pairs. Each pair selects one of the kinds of retreats discussed beginning on page 54 and pretends such a retreat has been held. Then one person asssumes the role of a newspaper reporter, and the other a person being interviewed. The reporter conducts the interview and prepares a news item which is approved by the interviewee. This is shared with the rest of the class. The news item must include statements about the purpose, goals, programming, and results or benefits of the retreat.

Have each class member write a letter of exhortation designed to get another person to attend a family camp. Put no restrictions or limitations on its content. Share letters in small groups.

Session Five
Special Groups

Divide your class into groups of two. Have one person invite the other to join a Christian Growth Group. Then reverse roles. Be sure Christian Growth Groups are explained and their benefits enumerated in the invitations.

Assume your class is a Christian Growth Group. Lead them in a study of Psalm 15 for ten minutes or so. Follow the suggestions on pages 64 to 66 for effective Bible study.

Typically, there are more single adults — post-high school to age ninety-nine — related to a local church than one supposes. Take an inventory for your church of such persons under the headings: never married, formerly married, and widowed.

Notice the nine needs of singles starting on page 67. Have each person rank these from most pressing to least pressing. Discuss individual rankings and than develop a ranking agreeable to most class members.

Invite a single adult to speak to your class for five minutes on the topic, "The Challenge of Being a Christian Single in Today's Society."

Arrange ahead of time to have a senior adult come to your class to be interviewed. As class teacher, serve as interviewer or get someone else to serve in that capacity. Through questioning bring out the senior adult's major concerns, fears, needs, and desires. Ask what he can do for the church, what the church can do for him, what attitude he wants others to have toward him, and what value he places on the church and its activities.

Take a poll of your class members. Give each three votes for the most attractive name for a senior's organization from those listed on page 75. Compile results to see which name(s) are preferred.

Session Six
Leadership Development

Ask each class member to write a one-sentence definition of leadership. Compare and discuss definitions. Then prepare a definition that most class members can agree to.

In groups of three, identify your church's greatest single personnel need. Then have groups list the characteristics needed in the person who would fill that position. Discuss each group's findings as an entire class.

Divide your class into groups of two. Have each group decide upon two leadership positions which need filling. Have the first person invite the second person to fill one position. Then have the second person invite the first to fill the other position. Encourage class members to study and practice the principles for making such invitations, beginning on page 84.

Obtain your denomination's handbook containing its leadership and service training program. (Write to the director of adult ministries at headquarters.) Present the major features of this program in the lecture/discussion format. Be sure to include how records are maintained, levels of certification, divisions of programs, and awards involved. Inform members how resources can be obtained. Explain any textbook series which may be a part of the program. Take your handbook to class and show it.

Have each class member consider his own history of leadership in the church. Then have each identify which of the nine support strategies beginning on page 88 had been used to keep him as a leader. Do the same for the twelve support ideas beginning on page 90. Discuss and compare answers as an entire class.